I0825498

Praise for
ALL RISE

"There is an immense amount of pressure in professional sports. If we fail, we go home and try again tomorrow. Rashmi was playing a different kind of game—one where failure didn't come with that option. Her story shows what true strength looks like when she was the only one left standing."

RAY ALLEN, **NBA Hall of Famer, philanthropist, and entrepreneur**

"Rashmi's story reveals the quiet pain so many people carry and the courage it takes to face ourselves with honesty and compassion. She shows how connection, accountability, and community can rebuild a life even in moments of profound isolation. *All Rise* is a reminder that healing is possible when we choose truth over fear and reach toward others instead of turning away. Her voice brings light to the places most people are afraid to name."

VIVEK MURTHY, **former United States surgeon general**

"In *All Rise*, Rashmi threads together the intricate questions of identity and the quiet peril of ambition—how a life built on achievement can become both armor and trap, a salve for the hidden ache of not feeling enough. She writes with rare honesty about the invisible weight women carry: the insistence that we be flawless, especially as mothers, and the unspoken warning that any misstep might mark us as unworthy, unwelcome, undone. Rashmi refuses that narrative. Instead, she insists on women's full dimensionality—our agency, our complexity, our right to falter and begin again. Her story is a powerful summons to befriend ourselves, to risk, to stumble, and to rise with the same fierce conviction that animates her own journey."

MOLLY BLOOM, **entrepreneur, speaker, and author of *Molly's Game***

"Rashmi delivers a rare blend of candor and insight that speaks to leaders at every level. *All Rise* is more than a memoir. It is a call to examine our choices, honor our values, and lead from a place of truth. Her journey shows that strength is built through accountability, humility, and the willingness to rise after every fall."

JEFFREY BARTEL, **chairman and managing director, Hamptons Group**

"Reading *All Rise* felt like sitting with a friend who refuses to let you shrink. Rashmi writes with warmth, vision, and a spirit that lifts you out of your own doubt. Her journey from heartbreak to healing gives every reader permission to choose purpose and walk toward a future filled with possibility."

SHANNON ALLEN, founder of Grown

"Rashmi's honesty moved me from the first page. She gives voice to the pressures many professionals feel but rarely acknowledge. *All Rise* is a powerful journey through accountability, renewal, and the strength that comes from owning your story. She reminds us that redemption is real and that purpose is built one brave step at a time."

DAMIEN ATKINS, former general counsel of Hershey's and current general counsel for MrBeast

"Rashmi brings humanity back into leadership in a way that feels urgently needed. Her story invites us to look at our own choices with humility and courage. *All Rise* shows how growth begins the moment we stop pretending and start listening to what our lives are trying to teach us. This book will stay with every leader who reads it."

ANDREW DAVIS, executive vice president and global chief people officer, Sony Music Entertainment

"*All Rise* is raw, real, and radically empowering. Rashmi's courage to turn her deepest shame into purpose gives every reader permission to face their own truth and rise through it."

MARSHALL GOLDSMITH, #1 *New York Times* bestselling author of *Triggers*, *What Got You Here Won't Get You There*, and *The Earned Life*

"This book is about redemption, but more than that, it's about responsibility. Rashmi's message reminds us that no matter how far we fall, we can always rise together and lift each other up with purpose and presence."

ALONZO MOURNING, NBA champion, philanthropist, and founder of the Mourning Family Foundation/Overtown Youth Center

"Rashmi's journey proves that success isn't about titles or money, it's about meaning. *All Rise* is a master class in resilience and the power of starting over with purpose."

JEFF HOFFMAN, cofounder of Priceline and Booking.com; chairman, Global Entrepreneurship Network

"Every entrepreneur needs to read this book. Rashmi turns adversity into insight and failure into fuel. Her honesty and authenticity are key components of the leadership model the world needs now."

Verne Harnish, founder of Entrepreneurs' Organization and author of *Scaling Up*

"Rashmi's story reminds us that humanity belongs in every boardroom and courtroom. *All Rise* is a wake-up call to every professional who has ever struggled with identity, ethics, or belonging."

LaTanya Langley, chief people officer, chief legal officer, and corporate secretary at Edgewell Personal Care

"From prison cell to purpose-driven leader, *All Rise* is a gutsy, unflinching journey of failure, truth, and ultimate triumph."

Laura Gassner Otting, *Wall Street Journal* bestselling author of *Wonderhell*

"Rashmi writes with a clarity that cuts through noise and reaches straight to the heart. She invites us into the moments that shaped her and shows how self-honesty can become a source of strength. *All Rise* is a powerful reminder that healing and leadership grow from the same soil when we choose courage over silence."

Minda Harts, author of *The Memo*

"Rashmi takes the reader on a breathtaking journey from rock bottom to radical self-awareness. It's an unforgettable story that reminds us that innovation starts within."

Josh Linkner, five-time tech entrepreneur, *New York Times* bestselling author of *Big Little Breakthroughs*, innovation keynote speaker, and venture capitalist

"Few leaders can articulate growth through failure like Rashmi does. Her insights are deeply human, yet profoundly strategic. This book belongs on every executive's shelf."

Narendra Kini, Chief Medical Officer, CDR Health and former CEO, Miami Children's Health System

"Rashmi's strength is contagious. *All Rise* isn't just a story about rebuilding, it's a movement for every woman who's ever doubted her power."

Monique Rodriguez, entrepreneur, philanthropist, and founder of Mielle Organics

"This book is a case study in courage. Rashmi dissects accountability, ego, and empathy with the precision of a scholar and the vulnerability of a survivor."

Alison Fragale, bestselling author of *Likeable Badass*, professor, and speaker

"Rashmi's story lit a spark in me. Her journey through loss, forgiveness, and renewal shows what's possible when we lead with heart instead of fear."

Steve O'Malley, Chief Operating Officer, Maritz

"'Everyone is doing it' is not a defense when you are the one held accountable. Rashmi's experience is a powerful reminder of vigilance in our standards and full ownership of our actions so we may heal and set an example for others."

Jeff Dudan, CEO, Homefront Brands

"Rashmi Airan's life—and this book—tell us how service, faith, and purpose can transform even the darkest chapters into legacies of light."

David Lawrence Jr., retired publisher of the *Miami Herald* and nationally known children's advocate

"Rashmi's story stayed with me long after I closed the book. Her honesty and deep reflection open a liminal space within you—one that lingers well beyond the page. It's the kind of pause we all need when examining how we're living, how we're moving through challenges, and how we choose to rise. *All Rise* captures a rare kind of transformation—one that reminds us why our authentic voices matter. Rashmi's will influence and impact many, inspiring us to step boldly into new action and shape lives that are truly transformative."

Mirjana Novkovic, founder of Speaker Story Bank and former VP of Marketing at the Harry Walker Agency

"Rashmi's story hits with the force of truth and the heart of a fighter. She shows what real grit looks like when the world stops cheering and you have to coach yourself through the hardest season of your life. *All Rise* is the kind of book that reminds you why courage matters and how strength is built one honest step at a time."

Dr. Jen Welter, NFL coach and trailblazer

A LAWYER'S EVOLUTION FROM PRISON TO PURPOSE

Rashmi Airan

www.amplifypublishinggroup.com

All Rise: A Lawyer's Evolution from Prison to Purpose

©2026 Rashmi Airan. All Rights Reserved. No part of this publication may be reproduced, stored in a retrieval system or transmitted in any form by any means electronic, mechanical, or photocopying, recording or otherwise without the permission of the author.

The views and opinions expressed in this book are solely those of the author. These views and opinions do not necessarily represent those of the publisher or staff. The advice and strategies found within may not be suitable for every situation. This work is sold with the understanding that neither the author nor the publisher is held responsible for the results accrued from the advice in this book. The publisher and the author assume no responsibility for errors, inaccuracies, omissions, or any other inconsistencies herein. All such instances are unintentional and the author's own.

For more information, please contact:
Amplify Publishing, an imprint of Amplify Publishing Group
620 Herndon Parkway, Suite 220
Herndon, VA 20170
info@amplifypublishing.com

Library of Congress Control Number: 2025925223

CPSIA Code: PRV0126A

ISBN-13: 979-8-89138-672-3

Printed in the United States

FOR KYLER AND MAYA

You have carried more than I ever dreamed life would ask of you, yet you emerged with hearts even stronger and spirits even brighter than I could have imagined. You are my light through every shadow, the pulse of my purpose, and the truest reason I continue to rise.

FOR MY PARENTS, DAR AND LALITA

Your love has been both anchor and horizon, holding me steady while reminding me where I am meant to go. Thank you for guiding me with wisdom, for challenging me toward truth, and for believing in me when I had forgotten how to believe in myself.

FOR MY SISTER, SUBHA

You have been my constant strength. Even as my younger sister, you led with courage, stood beside me through it all, and loved me without condition.

FOR MY SISTER, CATHERINE (ANGELI)

I felt your hand in every word I wrote. Your spirit and your gift with words live through these pages. You are still with me.

Contents

Introduction

I had the frame. I just didn't know how to live inside it.

I spent years chasing the perfect picture: the Ivy League education, the legal career, the happy family, the polished résumé, the community respect. I was checking every box, hitting every milestone, building an image of someone the world could admire.

From the outside, it looked flawless.

But inside, I was never satisfied. I wanted more. More success. More approval. More proof that I was enough. I told myself I was doing it all for my family, for my kids, for my husband, for our future. But the truth is, I was so busy creating the life I thought we should have that I wasn't actually living it.

I wasn't present.

I missed dinners. I missed laughter. I missed the little hands reaching for mine while I typed one more email. I missed the cracks forming quietly in my marriage. I missed the very moments that were supposed to matter most.

I was in the frame. But I wasn't in the moment.

And then the frame shattered.

When I went to federal prison, everything I thought defined me was stripped away. The titles. The approval. The illusion of control. I had no choice but to sit in the stillness and ask: Who am I now? Who was I ever, beyond the performance? And what does it mean to rise, not in spite of failure, but through it?

That's where this book begins.

Because it was never about the perfect picture. Not the carefully posed smiles. Not the curated moments with the right lighting and the perfect backdrop, designed to fit neatly inside a frame we can hang on the wall or post online.

The real story, the one that transforms us, is made up of the spaces in between. In the unspoken tension at the dinner table. In the tears we cry alone in the car. In the quiet pride of showing up even when we're breaking inside. In the conversations we have with ourselves when no one's watching.

And in the brave, messy, honest conversations we have with each other when we stop pretending. The pain, the joy, the shame, the love, that's what makes a life.

That's what belongs in the frame.

My name is Rashmi Airan, and I've lived the fall. I've watched the picture-perfect life collapse. I've faced the shame, the silence, and the long, painful reckoning of beginning again. But I also discovered something most of us never learn: When the image breaks, something true can finally begin.

This book is for the high-achievers who've spent their lives performing for the frame, chasing success, approval, and status, only to find themselves wondering what it's all for. It's for the leaders who always carry the weight, the parents rebuilding after a fall, the professionals who are so afraid to stop that they don't realize they've already lost themselves.

This isn't a book about resilience as you've heard it before. It's about what happens when the identity you built, your status, your so-called success, comes crashing down.

It's about the fear that keeps us chasing the next milestone, the next promotion, the next measure of worth without ever stopping to ask: What am I really running toward? Or what am I actually running from or hiding behind?

For those who have spent their lives proving themselves, whether in the boardroom, the courtroom, or their own minds, this book is a wake-up call. It dismantles the illusion that success equals security and forces us to confront the lies we tell ourselves about achievement, failure, and worth.

But this isn't just a reckoning. It's a road map. A process for rising through the inevitable struggles life throws our way. Because struggle isn't a detour; it's a doorway.

This book will strip away the noise and give you the tools to navigate adversity, to stand firm when everything else crumbles, and to build something real, something unshakable.

It's for anyone who's ever asked: What happens if I fail? Who am I without the achievement? What will they think if I lose it all?

This isn't a book about bouncing back. This isn't about returning to the image. It's about stepping out of the frame and into your life.

Through my story and the stories of others, I'll walk you through the RISE Framework®—a process I created through my own journey:

REFRAME: What if struggle isn't a detour but the way through?
IDENTIFY: Who are the people who will lift you, ground you, and hold up the mirror when you need it most?
SURRENDER: What if letting go of control is where real strength begins?
EVOLVE: How do you grow into the person you were meant to be, rooted in purpose, not performance?

And when we apply this process, something powerful happens. We stop pretending.

We build connection. We create belonging. We rise, together.

A few months ago, I found a photo of me and my family, back when the kids were just one and two. We're all smiling, radiant, the image of happiness. But I don't remember taking it. Not even a flicker of a memory. And that's what broke my heart most. I had worked so hard to build a life worth capturing . . . but I wasn't present enough to live it.

This book is my attempt to live in the frame now, not for the appearance of perfection, but for the messy, sacred truth of presence, purpose, and possibility.

Because the real test isn't whether we'll fall . . . it's whether we're ready to Rise Through It®.

How to Use This Book

This book is designed to be both a personal memoir and a leadership guide. Each chapter tells part of my story while offering practical insights for your own journey of transformation. Here's how to get the most from these pages:

START WHERE YOU ARE: You don't need to be in crisis to benefit from these principles. Whether you're facing change or a major setback, or simply seeking more authentic leadership, the RISE Framework can meet you where you are.

READ FOR CONNECTION: Allow yourself to connect emotionally with the narrative. Your circumstances may differ from mine, but the human experience of falling and rising is universal.

FOCUS ON THE FRAMEWORK: The RISE Framework that emerged from my journey provides a practical road map for navigating any challenge:

- **Reframe:** Shift your perspective to see challenges as catalysts rather than catastrophes.
- **Identify:** Connect with the people who ground you, lift you, and reflect truth back to you.
- **Surrender:** Let go of control, perfectionism, and resistance to embrace transformation.
- **Evolve:** Grow into your authentic self and purpose through intentional practice and presence.

IMPLEMENT THE TAKEAWAYS: Each chapter includes specific business applications that translate personal insights into organizational practices. These aren't theoretical concepts; they're battle-tested principles that work in the trenches of real leadership.

REFLECT ON THE QUESTIONS: Each chapter ends with reflection questions designed to help you apply the concepts to your own life and leadership. Consider journaling your responses or discussing them with trusted colleagues.

This book isn't meant to be read once and shelved. It's designed to be a companion on your ongoing journey of transformation. Dog-ear the pages that resonate. Highlight the passages that challenge you. Return to the reflections as your circumstances change.

Because rising isn't a one-time event; it's a continuous practice of becoming more authentic, more resilient, and more purposeful through whatever life brings your way.

Let's begin.

Prologue

The marble floor of the federal courthouse is cold and unforgiving as my knees buckle beneath me. I collapse, my body shaking uncontrollably as the judge's words echo through the packed courtroom: "One year and one day of incarceration."

The sentence reverberates in my chest. Around me, 180 of Miami's most respected attorneys, business leaders, and community members fill the courtroom benches. Many are crying. These are the people who once stood with me, who wrote letters about my character, who trusted me throughout my career as an attorney and community leader. And now, they are watching me fall.

I had built a successful legal practice in the heart of Miami's booming real estate market. I had worked late nights, closed difficult deals, and earned respect in rooms where I once felt invisible. In a single moment, all of it disintegrated. My reputation, my practice, my future.

I glance toward the front row. My parents sit rigid, their faces etched with the kind of pain I had sworn I would never cause them. It is the kind of pain that cannot be hidden, the kind that makes you feel small even as you try to stand tall.

Only moments earlier, I stood at the podium. I apologized to the court, to my family, and to my community. My words were heavy with remorse, but even as I said them, I knew they could never carry enough weight to undo the damage. Now, as the reality of the sentence crashes over me, one thought pierces through the fog of shame and shock.

What will happen to my children?

Kyler is ten. Maya is nine. How do you explain to your children that Mommy has to go to prison? How do you prepare them for the whispers at school, the empty chair at dinner, the nights when they cry for you and you can't be there? The questions slice through me more sharply than the sentence itself.

David, my attorney and friend, helps me to my feet. My body is trembling, but something unexpected steadies me. Out of nowhere, an image surfaces in my mind: my grandfather in a British prison cell in India in 1946.

I never met him. He died before I was born. But his story was woven into the fabric of my childhood. He had been imprisoned multiple times during India's fight for independence, each time returning home with stronger conviction that freedom and dignity mattered more than comfort.

If Dadaji could survive that, I can survive this.

The thought anchors me, even as my hands still shake. It is the first glimmer of something I would only come to recognize later: the seed of transformation. The truth is that sometimes strength is not about triumph, but about endurance. Sometimes purpose emerges only after everything else has been stripped away.

As I take my seat again, I cannot help but ask myself: How did I get here? How did a high-achieving attorney, a mother of two, end up in a federal courtroom, facing prison? The answer is not simple. It is a tangle of ambition, perfectionism, blind spots, and choices that built a life on the outside that looked flawless but was already cracking underneath.

My story begins with that immigrant drive for excellence, the relentless pursuit of achievement that defined my childhood and propelled me through an Ivy League education to early career success. It winds through the intoxicating years of the real estate boom in the mid-2000s, where the hunger to succeed clouded judgment and where opportunities too good to question became choices I would later regret.

But the real story is not about the fall.

It is about what happened after.

It is about the moment when the perfect picture I'd spent my life creating shattered completely, leaving me face-to-face with a question that would transform everything:

What if I stop performing for the frame and start being present with the people inside it?

That night, when I went home, I cried until I could not breathe. I leaned on my family with a desperation I had never allowed myself to show. I had no idea how I would live through the months ahead. I only knew I could not do it alone. What I did not know then was that this apparent ending would become a beginning. That the pain of being separated from my children would teach me more about presence and purpose than all my years of striving for achievement ever did. I only knew what my grandfather knew in that British prison cell, that rising through adversity is not just about surviving; it is about transforming.

What feels like breaking can become the beginning of becoming.

This is where my journey begins.

Prison Hack

PRISON ICED MOCHA COFFEE

INGREDIENTS

- 1 packet dark roast instant coffee (*commissary*)
- 1 packet powdered creamer (*commissary*)
- 6 sugar cubes (*commissary or chow hall sugar packets*)
- 1/4 cup chocolate milk (*kitchen or chow hall – often traded or saved from meals*)
- Ice (*from kitchen or saved from chow hall*)
- Hot water (*from microwave or sink*)

DIRECTIONS

1. Combine the instant coffee, powdered creamer, and sugar cubes in a cup.
2. Add a small amount of hot water to dissolve the mix. Microwave for 1 minute if needed.
3. Stir in the chocolate milk.
4. Add ice to chill the drink and enjoy your version of an iced mocha.

PART 1

Reframe

Reframing begins with the courage to see our circumstances differently. It asks us to shift our gaze, to stop seeing challenges as walls that block us and begin seeing them as doors that invite us into growth. At its core, reframing requires ownership and accountability. It is the moment we are brave enough to admit the role we have played in shaping our reality and the moment we accept the responsibility to choose how we will respond.

The chapters ahead reveal how this change in perspective can alter everything. It reshapes our relationship with uncertainty, adversity, and loss. What once felt like devastation can become the very thing that awakens us, the spark that forces us to change, the catalyst for a life we may never have imagined but desperately needed. The RISE Framework demands vulnerability. It is the strength to whisper, "This frame is no longer serving me," and the openness to step into a new one. It invites us to examine the stories we have rehearsed about success, failure, and worth, and to ask whether those stories are really true. Reframing is not denial, nor is it toxic positivity. It is the willingness to sit inside the struggle and uncertainty long enough to find meaning, to uncover the possibility hidden inside the pain, and to trust that the wisdom we need is waiting for us there. And perhaps most of all, reframing requires faith. Faith when the path forward is clouded. Faith when the ground beneath us feels shattered. I learned this on that courthouse floor, when I had nothing left to cling to but trust. In those moments, when life feels stripped bare, we are often being prepared for a purpose we cannot yet see.

The chapters in this section explore how that shift from "this is happening to me" to "this is happening for me" becomes the foundation of growth. It is what allows us to rise through our inevitable falls not with bitterness, but with grace. To confront uncertainty as a doorway to what is greater on the other side not with fear, but with purpose. Not with performance for the frame, but with the courage to finally live inside the life that is ours.

CHAPTER 1

The Blueprint

Leaders are not born in moments of triumph. They are forged in fire, shaped by the people who came before them, and defined by how they rise when everything falls apart. My leadership began long before a courtroom or a prison cell. It began in the stories of my ancestors, in the stubborn faith of immigrants, in the courage of ordinary people standing inside extraordinary storms.

YOUR INHERITED BLUEPRINT MATTERS

My grandfather was Banarsi Das Saraf. My *dadaji.* A freedom fighter in India's struggle against the British alongside Mahatma Gandhi. On the day that my dad was born in 1946, my *dadaji* was sitting in a jail cell because of the revolution. He was released, ate with his wife and nine children, then returned to the fight. In time there would be twelve children. Conviction did not rest. The cell that held him was built to break men. A room meant for four often held twelve. The floor stayed wet with monsoon seepage. Light entered through a narrow slit that only hinted at the passing of days. The British believed discomfort would crush resolve. They did not understand that discomfort ends and conviction does not.

So my dad grew up inside uncertainty. His father's health failed from repeated imprisonments. India finally won its freedom, yet my family did not know if my grandfather would survive. The family jewelry business faltered in the economic shock that followed independence. Fear sat with them in their rural village of Beri.

When my dad was twelve, he came home in his khaki school uniform, slate tucked under his arm, and my grandfather said, "Let's go for a bike ride." My grandfather could not ride because of emphysema, so he sat in the small carriage attached to my dad's bicycle. They pedaled along dirt roads to a pond, picked fruit from the trees, and sat down to eat.

My dad had just finished Gandhi's autobiography. In it, Gandhi shares a deeply embarrassing moment from his life. My dad asked, "Why would he include something so shameful for the entire world to read forever?"

My grandfather answered, "That is the point. When you live through hard lessons and emerge with strength, you carry a responsibility to share so others do not repeat your errors."

I am living that lesson. I am his legacy. I do not hide my fall. I share it, not in spite of shame but because of what it taught me. Our greatest value to others often rises from how we stand back up after we fall.

In 1967 my dad crossed the Atlantic with eight dollars and a promise to his family to return. He worked, studied, and sent money home. At one point he held three jobs while attending school. He saved enough to buy a tractor and have it delivered to our village for the family sugarcane side business.

This is the blueprint I inherited. Integrity, resilience, and the obligation to turn failure into wisdom. These values became part of me before I learned their names. Every leader carries an unseen blueprint. Until you recognize the stories that shaped you, you unconsciously lead from them. **Self-awareness is not optional. It is a leadership imperative.**

CULTURAL INTELLIGENCE STARTS AT HOME

My earliest story of my mom is about her journey to America, which began with a trick, one that would ultimately change her life and mine. At just eighteen years old, my mom, Lalita, had already accomplished what few women of her generation had, completing a master's degree in economics. Her professors spoke of her potential for doctoral studies, and she dreamed of attending the London School of Economics.

During her final exams, she received an urgent call from her father. Her mother was gravely ill, and she needed to come home immediately. Without hesitation, Mom jumped on the next train, traveling three and a half hours to Rewari, her hometown.

When she arrived, she discovered the truth. There was no illness. Her family had engineered the ruse to bring her home to meet a potential suitor, a young engineer who had been studying in America.

This was my father, Damodar.

My mother was furious. She had no interest in an arranged marriage, particularly not one that would interrupt her studies and derail her professional ambitions. When she was asked to sit down with my father, she decided to be deliberately difficult.

"Do you have a problem going with me to America?" my father asked, following the traditional script of these arranged marriage meetings.

My mother's response was anything but traditional. "It doesn't matter to me either way," she replied with deliberate indifference. "If you're going to jump in a well, it doesn't really matter which well you're jumping in."

Her calculated defiance, intended to discourage this potential match, had the opposite effect. After meeting nine other potential brides who had eagerly tried to impress him with their willingness to move to America, my father was intrigued by this brilliant, rebellious woman who couldn't care less about his American dreams.

Three days later, they were engaged. Two weeks after that, they were married. One month after their wedding, my mother left everything she knew, her family, her dreams, her culture, to follow my father to a country she'd never seen.

This arranged meeting that unexpectedly became a love story taught me that sometimes what appears to be resistance can ultimately lead to a greater purpose. My mother's rebellious spirit didn't prevent her fate; it shaped it. Her strength didn't diminish in marriage but found new expression.

Cultural intelligence starts at home. Understanding your own cultural inheritance is the foundation for navigating differences with authenticity and empathy. My mother's ability to transfer her strength, intelligence, and adaptability into a completely new context is a perfect example of this. **Leaders who embrace the complexity of their**

heritage can understand differences, adapt across contexts, and lead with deeper empathy than those who ignore their cultural roots.

So my parents then immigrated to the US with this one simple belief: that with hard work and determination, they would make it. They could achieve that coveted American Dream.

STRATEGY IS BORN FROM STRUGGLE

The frame of my life began taking shape long before I was born. My grandfather's imprisonment during India's fight for independence, my parents' journey across oceans with eight dollars and boundless determination, these became the edges of the picture I felt destined to fill. As the eldest daughter of immigrants, I inherited not just their dreams but their unspoken expectations: that I would validate their sacrifices by creating a life worthy of framing, a success story that would justify leaving everything they knew behind.

They pursued master's and doctorate degrees. They were entrepreneurs and started their own engineering consulting firm. Later, they adapted to the market and started a real estate investment and syndication business.

I was born Rashmi, which means the rays of the morning sun.

Most of my childhood memories center around gathering at one or another auntie and uncle's house. But I was conflicted. I was living in an Indian home in an immigrant community but trying to be as American as I could. I wanted to be more Western than my Indian friends. I grew up a nerd; I was unpopular, overweight, and often the brunt of jokes and ridicule.

Internally, I felt so much pressure to "succeed." I was in a communal struggle with the rest of my immigrant community to achieve, to prove myself in the Western society in a way that would make my family and community proud, to essentially validate that the move across the ocean to a new country was worth it.

And I wanted to know that I accomplished that goal, that my parents' sacrifices and efforts ultimately had value. I sought awards, competitions, medals, and accolades with fury and gusto.

And make no mistake, there was no sense that I was being pressured to be this way; in fact, I knew it was an unspoken duty. To make my parents, my community, and ultimately my extended family in India proud. It didn't seem like a chore but rather a privilege to be able to work hard.

I am the oldest of three girls in the family. As a young girl, it was very obvious that a traditional Indian family places value, reputation, and emphasis on having a boy in the family. But my dad loved having three girls! He used to say, "I love being the only man in the house!" Even though my parents received a lot of pressure from family members in India to keep trying for a boy, my parents let everyone know that they had no intention of trying to condone this belief. They made it clear that they saw boys and girls as equal.

But here's the thing: I do believe that as my parents' eldest child, I felt pressure to be the perfect child, to be strong like the son they never had. I vowed to be independent and persistent, to never be weak, and to take on any task. I wanted to prove to myself that a girl was equal to a boy, not only in academics and a career but also personally and in life.

I thought if I asked for help with anything, I would be perceived as weak and that I had failed to attain perfection and validate my parents' conviction that girls can do anything.

So I was the girl who understood and believed that I could do anything I put my mind to.

But deep inside, my entire self-worth, value, and esteem was rooted in my achievements. I didn't understand self-love. The only reason I believed people would love me was because of my grades. The awards I won. The accolades I received.

I didn't think people actually liked me for me, even my friends, and I have incredible friends from those years who are still my best friends. But I always felt like I was vying for their love and friendship, never truly believing I deserved it.

Years later, when I entered the corporate world, I'd see this same pattern in other high-achieving professionals, the relentless need to prove their worth through achievement, the inability to separate their performance from their value as human beings. What had served us well in school and early in our careers would eventually become the very thing that limited our growth and authenticity as leaders.

Both Mom and Dad were risk-takers, and every business venture they started was laced with it. I watched my parents work nonstop, but they never seemed to be worried about how they would take care of us. My mom and dad always showed such faith that they would always be able to use their minds and education to earn income.

This unwavering confidence in their ability to create opportunity from knowledge became a foundational belief in our household. They didn't just work hard; they worked smart, constantly adapting and learning. When one business venture didn't pan out, they pivoted. When markets shifted, they evolved. Their entrepreneurial spirit wasn't just about making money; it was about proving that intelligence and determination could overcome any obstacle.

Watching them navigate uncertainty with such grace taught me that security doesn't come from having all the answers; it comes from trusting your ability to find solutions when challenges arise. This lesson would prove invaluable later in my life, when I faced my own seemingly insurmountable obstacles and had to rebuild from nothing.

Strategy is born from struggle. Innovation doesn't always come from boardrooms and high-powered strategy sessions. Sometimes it emerges from necessity, from the creative problem-solving required when resources are scarce and stakes are high. The strategic thinking developed in these crucibles often provides a competitive edge that can't be taught in business schools.

REWRITE THE NARRATIVE, DON'T REJECT IT

In 1989, my senior year in high school, my parents lost everything, and we were forced to file for bankruptcy and lost our home to foreclosure. I watched my parents closely. Even though the real estate market had collapsed and my parents really couldn't have done anything different to save their real estate assets, it was painful. My dad has told me many times that he would go into his bathroom and cry in his bathtub, away from Mom and us three girls, because he felt like he had failed.

Losing money and filing for bankruptcy are seen as failures in our society. Dad and Mom felt like they had let so many people down.

But they kept their faith, love in the home, and a positive attitude with the confidence to try again. Not only did I have my grandfather as an example, but I also had my parents, who proved they were fighters and survivors too.

Like their own parents, they dared to be great again and to take another risk. They picked themselves up and hung out their shingle; Dad started practicing law, and Mom started a business. Wait, here is the most incredible thing from that part of our lives. In the bankruptcy, my parents' financial obligations legally dissolved.

But my parents had given their word. They had shaken hands with friends, family, and others and personally guaranteed each investment. That is how much they believed in what they were doing.

So, for the past twenty-five years since filing for bankruptcy, my parents have upheld their personal guarantees and have slowly made payments to their creditors each year to satisfy what they believe is their moral obligation to make those investors whole. To date, they have paid back about $1 million without being legally obligated to do so.

That choice shaped me. Relationships are sacred. Your word matters.

Rewrite the narrative; don't reject it. True leadership is about reframing your difficulties and challenges as fuel for a bold vision. My parents didn't let bankruptcy define them as failures. Instead, they reframed it as an opportunity to demonstrate their deepest values of integrity and resilience. They transformed what could have been a legacy of shame into a powerful example of character.

During all this, we had no money for college. I was about to graduate from high school, and I knew that my college education would be a source of financial stress for my parents. So, during my senior summer, I began to sell Cutco knives.

It was then, at the age of seventeen, that I learned my true skills: building relationships, making presentations, public speaking, and selling. I won every sales award that summer. I made enough money to pay for college after financial aid.

I learned more about persuasion, resilience, and human psychology in those three months selling knives door-to-door than I did in many of my college courses. Each rejection was a lesson. Each successful sale was confirmation that I could create value and connection even in brief encounters.

This experience became another thread in my leadership tapestry, the understanding that influence isn't about position but about the ability to create meaningful connection and demonstrate authentic value.

When I arrived at UNC Chapel Hill in the fall of 1989, I was determined to shed the awkward, overweight, high-school version of myself and create something new. I joined a sorority, threw myself into the Campus Y and nonprofit work, and became active in student government. For the first time in my life, I felt like I could be both a serious student and a social being.

I made incredible friends during those years, friendships that have lasted decades. There was something magical about that time and place, the way we could debate philosophy over terrible coffee and still laugh until our stomachs hurt. I studied relentlessly, but I also experienced the joy of community in ways I never had before. Chapel Hill will be forever my Happy Place.

My academic focus was communications, specializing in rhetoric, and I was also working toward a minor in business administration. I wrote my entire honors thesis at Columbia Street Bakery. I was never a library girl; I needed the energy of people around me, the hum of conversation and life. The coffee was subpar, but every night I'd meet my friend Dana and others there. We'd create this little community of students, working and studying together until late. And every single night, I'd reward myself with a trip to the Yogurt Pump (now called YoPo) for my favorite frozen yogurt treat.

Those years weren't just about academics. I saw incredible concerts: the Grateful Dead, James Taylor, the Indigo Girls. Music became another way to connect with this new version of myself, this young woman who was learning to embrace both her heritage and her American dreams.

One summer, I interned for Senator Bob Graham, the US senator from Florida, working in his DC legislative office as an aide. Being in the halls of power, seeing how policy was made and how voices could influence change, planted seeds that would influence my understanding of leadership for years to come.

But beneath the surface of my seemingly successful college experience, a darker pattern was emerging. The same drive for perfection that fueled my academic achievements and leadership ambitions began to consume me in dangerous ways.

I had always struggled with my weight and body image, feeling too big, too different from the slender ideal I saw around me. But by my junior year, my desire to finally achieve the "perfect" body had spiraled into something much more serious. I was anorexic, though I didn't recognize it at the time.

I began avoiding meals with friends, making excuses about being too busy studying or having already eaten. I'd exercise at odd hours, late at night or very early in the morning, when no one would notice how obsessive my routines had become. I was hardly eating, surviving on coffee, diet sodas, and the occasional piece of fruit. The frozen yogurt trips to the Yogurt Pump became my one "allowed" indulgence, but even then, I'd feel guilty afterward.

My friends at Columbia Street Bakery would invite me to grab dinner, and I'd always have an excuse. "I already ate," or "I'm not hungry," or "I need to finish this paper first." The truth was, I was terrified of food, terrified of losing control, terrified that if I ate normally, I'd go back to being the overweight, ridiculed girl from high school.

Thankfully, two of my closest friends, Jennifer and Meredith, recognized what was happening before I did. They staged an intervention, literally taking me to UNC Health Services and insisting I get help. I'll never forget sitting in that counselor's office, finally hearing the words "eating disorder" applied to my behavior.

It was one of the most humbling moments of my young life. Here I was, someone who prided herself on being smart, disciplined, and in control, and I had to admit that I had lost control entirely. I had to learn about nutrition from scratch, not as a diet or a restriction but as nourishment. I had to understand how to balance food, exercise, and health in ways that sustained rather than depleted me.

The recovery process taught me something crucial about perfectionism that would serve me throughout my life: The very traits that can drive success can also become self-destructive when taken to extremes. The same attention to detail that made me a good student had turned into an obsession with counting calories. The same discipline that helped me excel academically had become a rigid control that was slowly killing me.

This experience also taught me about the power of true friendship. Jennifer and Meredith didn't enable my behavior or ignore the warning signs because it was uncomfortable to address. They loved me enough to intervene, even when it was awkward and difficult. They showed me that real community means caring enough to speak hard truths.

Recovery wasn't quick or easy, but it was essential. Learning to nourish my body properly became a metaphor for learning to nourish my whole self, not just with achievements and accolades but with genuine self-care, authentic relationships, and a more balanced understanding of what it means to be successful.

During my junior year at UNC Chapel Hill, around the same time I was working through my eating disorder recovery, I decided to run for student body president, the only woman in a field of men. This was a formative leadership moment for me, rooted in both courage and cultural narrative.

My campaign wasn't just about winning an election; it was about challenging assumptions about who could lead and how. I brought together a diverse coalition of students, focusing on issues that affected marginalized communities often overlooked by student government.

I lost by seven votes. Yes, seven.

That number haunted me. It was small enough to make me wonder about every conversation I had, every flyer I handed out, every step I took. For days it felt like my entire worth had been reduced to a single digit.

And yet, even in defeat, I discovered impact.

I went on to establish one of my main platform ideas, the Peer Advising Counseling Program, which UNC did not have at the time, and worked alongside Dean Don Boulton, the dean of students. And today, the Peer Advising Counseling Program is still active and assisting students daily! The sting of loss has softened into pride that I created something lasting.

That loss shaped my understanding of leadership. Power is not always a position. Sometimes it is the conversation you change and the doors you open. My strength was not in mirroring male models. It was in collaboration, inclusion, and lifting as I climbed.

For my honors thesis, I chose to write about the Chipko Andolan, the grassroots movement that started in the foothills of India with village women fighting developers who wanted to cut down trees in the Himalayas. These women understood that deforestation would directly harm their villages and children. Their movement became the genesis of the tree-hugging protests that Greenpeace would later adopt worldwide.

The thesis I wrote connected the Chipko Andolan women and my experience running for student body president in ways I didn't fully understand at the time. Both experiences were about finding a voice in the face of systems that didn't naturally make space for you. Both were about understanding that real change often starts at the grassroots level, with people who are willing to stand up and say, "This matters, and I'm going to do something about it."

The summer before my senior year, my friend Josh, who's arguably like a brother to me, took me to New York City for the first time. He opened up a whole new world: my first Broadway show, Central Park, SoHo, Times Square, Rockefeller Center. Walking through those streets, I felt the pull of possibility, the sense that maybe I could make it in places that had once seemed impossibly far for a little Indian girl from Miami.

Those late nights at Columbia Street Bakery, surrounded by friends who believed in me even when I didn't quite believe in myself, taught me that community isn't just about shared background; it's about shared purpose and mutual support. The leadership lessons I learned at Carolina, about authentic voice, the power of intervention when someone you love is struggling, and turning defeat into lasting change, would serve me throughout my career, even when everything else fell apart.

Years later, when I would face my legal troubles and eventual imprisonment, I would draw on these lessons about perfectionism, control, and the importance of accepting help when you need it. The eating disorder was my first real confrontation with the fact that my greatest strengths could become my greatest weaknesses when left unchecked. And the campaign loss taught me that impact isn't always measured by the position you hold, but by the change you create and the doors you open for others.

The threads of struggle, resilience, identity, and imperfection didn't unravel my story; they rewrote it into something stronger. **True leadership isn't born from erasing the past, but from transforming it into purpose, power, and presence.**

My grandfather's words echo across generations: *When you go through life's hard lessons and come out with strength and hard-fought lessons, you have a responsibility to share it so that others will not make the same errors that you made.*

This is my responsibility now. This is my leadership. This is the gift I offer to everyone I serve.

LEADERSHIP LESSONS: YOUR ORIGIN STORY INFORMS YOUR LEADERSHIP

1. **Your inherited blueprint matters.** The values, beliefs, and behaviors you observed growing up create unconscious patterns in your leadership approach. Recognizing these patterns gives you the power to choose which elements to embrace and which to transform.

2. **Cultural intelligence starts at home.** Understanding your own cultural inheritance is the foundation for navigating difference with authenticity and empathy. Your unique cultural perspective can become a leadership advantage rather than a liability.
3. **Strategy is born from struggle.** Some of the most innovative business approaches emerge not from abundance but from necessity. The constraints and challenges in your background may have equipped you with strategic thinking that others lack.
4. **Rewrite the narrative, don't reject it.** True leadership isn't about denying your roots; it's about reframing them as fuel for a bold vision. Your inherited stories don't have to be your destiny; they can be the raw material from which you craft something new.

REFLECTION QUESTIONS

- How have your origin story, your family history, cultural background, and early experiences influenced your leadership approach? What patterns can you identify?
- What values were emphasized in your family growing up, and how do these show up in your decision-making today? Which serve you well, and which might need reexamination?
- What is the legacy you want to leave through your leadership? How does it connect to the values and lessons from your background?

CHAPTER 2

The Illusion of Success Is a Trap

Landing a job at Morgan Stanley in investment banking fresh out of college felt like I had made the immigrant dream come true. I remember my first day, walking into the imposing glass tower in Manhattan, my carefully selected navy suit a badge of belonging. My heart raced with a mixture of pride and terror. Would they discover I didn't belong? Would they see through my carefully constructed facade of confidence?

SUCCESS WITHOUT ALIGNMENT IS EMPTY

I was part of a pool of about eighty financial analysts, the top of the top from some of the best schools across the country. Harvard, Princeton, Yale, Stanford, UNC, Michigan, Rice, we were the cream of the crop, now suddenly reduced to peons in the Morgan Stanley hierarchy. We had signed up for a grueling two-year investment banking program that would test every limit we thought we had.

The corporate finance division was a machine designed to extract maximum productivity from brilliant young minds. We worked one-hundred-hour weeks, every single week, for two straight years. No vacations. Hardly any sleep. The pace was relentless, analyzing financial models until my eyes burned, preparing pitch books until dawn, flying across the country for client meetings on a moment's notice.

Everyone seemed to move with purpose, speak with authority, and know exactly what they were doing. I mimicked their confidence, their language, their mannerisms. I stayed late, arrived early, and volunteered for the assignments no one wanted. I was determined to prove I belonged in this elite circle.

We worked hard, but we also played hard. Late-night dinners at expensive restaurants after closing deals. Weekend trips to the Hamptons when we could steal away. Somehow, I still found the energy to work out at the gym at 2:00 a.m. and occasionally meet friends for drinks that stretched until sunrise, running on pure adrenaline and ambition.

The money was intoxicating. When my first bonus check arrived, I called my father immediately.

"Dad, you won't believe how much they're paying me," I said, my voice shaking with excitement. "I'm so proud of you," he replied. I could hear the tears in his voice.

That moment should have been pure joy, validation of all my hard work, all my parents' sacrifice. Instead, it was tinged with something else: the creeping realization that I was measuring my worth by the size of my paycheck. The bigger the number, the more valuable I was.

This wasn't just a career choice; it was becoming my identity.

But even as the money rolled in and the prestige accumulated, something fundamental was missing. Despite learning an enormous amount about finance, markets, and dealmaking, I felt spiritually empty. The work wasn't fulfilling, even though I knew I could make a lot of money if I stayed on this path. Each successful transaction felt hollow; each client interaction felt transactional rather than meaningful.

When your drive comes from needing to prove yourself, to parents, peers, or society, it clouds judgment and opens the door to ethical compromise. This pattern of "proving" doesn't just affect individual decision-making; it shapes organizational cultures where appearance outweighs substance and short-term wins eclipse long-term integrity.

I was caught in this trap, constantly needing to demonstrate my value through achievement. Each success raised the bar for the next, creating an exhausting cycle of striving without satisfaction. This need to prove myself wasn't just personally draining; it was professionally dangerous.

After those intense years at Morgan Stanley, I made a pivotal decision. Investment banking wasn't giving me the sense of purpose I craved. Fortunately, I had received a two-year deferral from Columbia Law School before taking the Morgan Stanley position, knowing even then that I might want to explore a different path. Now that deferral felt like a lifeline.

Columbia Law School represented a complete shift from the corporate finance world. I had gone from analyzing spreadsheets and structuring deals to studying constitutional law and human rights.

For the first time in years, I could breathe.

My first year, I sort of relaxed after those very hard two years at Morgan Stanley. I was a student again, not a cog in an efficiency machine. I took classes that excited me: human rights law, equal protection, constitutional theory. I developed close relationships with professors like John Manning, Louis Henkin, and Kimberlé Crenshaw, who opened my mind to new ways of thinking about justice, equality, and the law's role in society.

Professor Crenshaw's work on intersectionality particularly resonated with me as I grappled with my own identity as an Indian American woman in predominantly white spaces. Her classes on equal protection showed me how the law could be a tool for systemic change, not just individual advancement.

After that first year of adjustment, I hunkered down and worked really hard. I became the articles editor for the *Human Rights Law Review*, pouring my energy into scholarship that felt meaningful. Unlike the financial models I'd created at Morgan Stanley, these articles explored questions that mattered, how the law could protect the vulnerable, advance justice, create a more equitable society.

I sang in the Columbia Law Revue with my best friend Meredith, finding joy in creative expression that had been completely absent from my banking days. We would go to Broadway shows, sometimes alone, sometimes together, losing ourselves in stories that explored the full range of human experience. We attended concerts and wandered through SoHo and the West Village, and I rediscovered parts of myself that had been dormant during those grueling years of financial modeling.

By my third year, I was named a Kent Scholar, the highest honor awarded to a Columbia Law student. When I was chosen to be the emcee of our law school graduation at Carnegie Hall, I felt a pride that was different from any bonus check or deal closing. This was recognition not just of my academic achievement but of my leadership, my voice, and my ability to connect with others.

Standing on that stage at Carnegie Hall, looking out at my classmates and their families, I felt like I was finally on the right path. Law felt like a calling, not just a career. The intersection of my analytical skills from Morgan Stanley and my newfound passion for justice seemed to create unlimited possibilities.

Upon graduation, I accepted a position at Orrick, Herrington & Sutcliffe, a prestigious law firm in San Francisco. The West Coast felt like a fresh start, an opportunity to use my legal education in service of something larger than profit maximization.

I worked there for about a year, but something didn't feel right. Despite the prestige and compensation, despite doing work that was intellectually challenging, I felt a growing need to be closer to my parents, to return to my roots. So I made the decision to move back to Miami, prioritizing family connection over professional advancement, one of the few times I listened to my inner compass rather than external metrics of success.

My professional journey in Miami began at a small litigation boutique. I was excited about the opportunity to gain hands-on experience in a smaller setting, to really learn the practice of law rather than just its theory. But my enthusiasm quickly faded as I encountered a toxic environment where men had unfair advantages and inappropriate sexual behavior was tolerated. The misalignment between my values and this culture became impossible to ignore, and I made the difficult decision to leave.

My next role was at the Miami-Dade County Attorney's Office, where I represented the mayor, commissioners, and various departments. Initially, the work felt meaningful: I was serving the public, using my legal skills to address community needs. This felt closer to the justice-oriented work I had dreamed about in Professor Crenshaw's classes.

But as I quickly mastered my assigned departments and asked for more challenging work, I was turned down. There were no mentors looking out for me, no one investing in my growth. The assignments were siloed, with one attorney handling each matter in isolation. I found myself bored, unchallenged, and professionally stagnated. The bureaucracy that I thought would serve justice seemed more interested in maintaining the status quo.

Shortly after moving back to Miami, I started dating Erik, a firefighter who lived his life in service of others. He was completely different from anyone in my family or community, and he made me laugh in ways I hadn't experienced before. While my world revolved around achievements and accolades, his centered on showing up for people in their worst moments, saving lives, and protecting communities.

We dated for a few years, and in 2002, while I was still at the county attorney's office, we got married. Kyler arrived in 2004, followed by Maya in 2006. On paper, it looked like the dream. The accomplished attorney and the heroic firefighter. Two beautiful children. A home in Pinecrest. From the outside, we were the picture of stability, the kind of family people admired and envied.

Inside, though, I was slipping further into a pattern that had ruled me for years. Perform. Achieve. Prove. I believed that if I just worked harder and climbed higher, I would finally arrive at a place where I could rest, where presence would come easily. That day never came.

The frenzy of constant striving seeped into our marriage in quiet but devastating ways. Erik longed for a partner who could sit with him at the end of a long shift and truly be there, who could laugh with him over a simple dinner or watch the children play without looking past the moment. What he got instead was someone always half absent, my body at the table but my mind already chasing the next client, the next deal to close, the next accolade to secure.

The walls of our home should have held laughter, warmth, and ease, yet too often they echoed with my absence. Erik's presence was steady, rooted in the life we were building, while mine was scattered, split between the people who mattered most and the validation I thought I still had to earn. I told myself I was doing it all for our family, for our future. The truth was harder to face. I did not yet know how to choose being over doing.

I remember cradling Kyler as an infant, his tiny chest rising and falling against mine, while my mind wandered to the closing I had to prepare for. I remember holding Maya's hand as we sat together, but even then, part of me was already somewhere else, calculating what came next. Those were sacred moments, yet I let them slip by under the weight of proving myself.

What Erik deserved, and what my children deserved, was not the woman who kept adding to her résumé. They deserved the woman who could stop, breathe, and stay present with them in the ordinary holiness of our everyday life.

BEWARE THE COST OF PROVING

When success becomes your primary identity, relationships become secondary priorities. I told myself I was building this life for our family, but I wasn't actually building a life with them. I was constructing an image of family success while missing the daily intimacy that makes a marriage thrive.

The communication between Erik and I became increasingly toxic. We started fighting more and connecting less. I realize now that my obsessive focus on the frame, on how our life looked from the outside, contributed highly to the eventual demise of our marriage. I struggled to be personally present for the people I loved most.

The irony wasn't lost on me: The firefighter who ran toward danger to save strangers was married to someone who ran toward achievement to avoid the vulnerability of true intimacy.

I knew I needed a change in my career. I wanted to create something of my own, to use my legal education and financial background in a more direct way. So I took a leap of faith and started my own law practice, focusing on real estate transactions.

Starting my own law practice as a real estate attorney felt like the ultimate win. I was my own boss, creating my own schedule, building something from nothing. The early days were exhilarating: setting up my small office in a modest two-story building, part of a strip of professional offices just half a mile from my home, designing my letterhead, signing my first clients. I felt a sense of ownership and purpose that had been missing in my previous roles.

But as the practice grew, so did the pressure. The overhead costs mounted: staff salaries, office rent, insurance, software. Each month brought new financial obligations that required more revenue, more clients, more hours. What had started as a dream of independence became another treadmill.

These competing desires created a tension I couldn't resolve. I told myself I was working these long hours for them, to secure their future. But each missed dinner, each bedtime I wasn't there for, each weekend spent catching up on work instead of building memories, these accumulated into an absence I couldn't justify.

I was caught in a common trap: mistaking providing for parenting. Yes, my children needed financial security. But they also needed me, my presence, my attention, my guidance. No amount of material comfort could compensate for a missing parent.

MISALIGNMENT MASKS AS OPPORTUNITY

In the fall of 2007, I ran into an old colleague from the Miami-Dade County Attorney's Office at a restaurant in Coconut Grove. PT wasn't a close friend, more of an acquaintance, but she mentioned she knew a developer looking for a new closing attorney.

"They're doing really innovative things with buyer incentives," she said. "Creative but legal. They need someone who can handle volume and complexity."

I felt a flutter of excitement. This could be it, the big client that would solve my growing financial pressures, the volume business that would provide stability, leading to more time with my kids.

Looking back, I can now see clearly what I chose to ignore then: I saw a big client as the solution to all my problems. I reframed red flags as opportunity and paid the price.

The developer's office in North Miami Beach was ordinary, just a simple conference room with no views, nothing lavish or particularly impressive. I noticed the yarmulkes worn by the operations team, and something in me relaxed. These were religious men; surely their ethics would be beyond reproach.

ER, the operations director, laid out their approach. The developer was offering rental guarantees to buyers, managing the properties, and creating what he described as win-win situations for everyone involved. The structure was complex but seemed legitimate. They'd been working with a large law firm but wanted someone more . . . nimble.

"Why are you leaving your current firm?" I asked, the question arising from some deeply buried instinct for self-protection.

"They're too slow, too bureaucratic," ER explained smoothly. "We need someone who can move at our pace, who understands our vision."

I nodded, flattered by the implication that I was more agile, more visionary than a large, established firm. What I didn't ask was whether that firm had raised concerns about their practices, whether "bureaucratic" was code for "asking too many questions."

When misalignment meets opportunity, our capacity for self-deception is remarkable. We see what we want to see, hear what we want to hear, and believe what we need to believe to justify the path of least resistance. This isn't just a personal failing; it's a pattern that plays out in businesses and organizations everywhere.

I called my title insurance underwriter, explaining the transactions but, I now realize, emphasizing the aspects that would gain approval while minimizing the elements that might raise concerns. I told myself I wasn't lying. I was just focusing on the relevant parts.

The first closings began to roll in. The volume was staggering, the complexity challenging. I threw myself into creating perfect systems, flawless documentation. My staff expanded. Revenue began to soar. Finally, I was achieving at the level I'd been groomed for all my life.

But there were moments, small, quiet moments, when something felt off. A realtor would make a comment about payments happening outside closing. A buyer would seem confused about the rental guarantee structure. Each time, I would push the doubt away, focus on the documentation, on keeping my files perfect.

In hindsight, I can now see that every step, from investment banking to law school to my own practice, was both a triumph and a trap. Each achievement pulled me further from my core values while convincing me I was on the right path. Each success made it harder to course-correct, to admit I might have taken a wrong turn.

It was soon Christmas Eve 2007. The house was filled with family, the scent of holiday cookies mixing with the pine aroma from our tree. Christmas music played softly in the background. The kids were finally going to bed, and I should have been enjoying this rare moment of peace with our extended family.

Instead, I was sitting in the glider in my children's room, singing my nightly lullaby and trying to make them sleep while checking emails on my Blackberry. The message from the realtor was simple, just a line about a buyer receiving funds from a rental guarantee, with an attachment.

I forwarded it to my closing coordinator without opening the attachment. A small decision. A tiny choice. The kind of moment that doesn't feel decisive when you're living it.

PRESENCE IS THE RAREST CURRENCY

I was always there, but not really there. I was chasing the next goal, the next deal, the next win. Physically present but mentally absent, reviewing documents in my head during my son's soccer game, composing emails while bathing my daughter, checking messages during family dinners.

I thought I was doing it for my family, but I wasn't fully with them. Success had become my distraction.

I justified the long hours, the missed moments, the exhaustion, telling myself I was building a better life. But was I? What is the value of a beautiful home if you're rarely in it? What is the point of financial security if it comes at the cost of connection?

Presence isn't just a personal virtue; it's a professional one. Leaders who are fully present make better decisions, build stronger teams, and create more sustainable businesses. They listen more carefully, observe more accurately, and respond more appropriately. They create cultures of engagement rather than exhaustion.

My inability to be fully present wasn't just hurting my family; it was compromising my professional judgment. I was too busy looking ahead to the next deal to notice the warning signs in the current one. I was too focused on growth to question whether that growth was healthy.

That's what breaks my heart the most. I had worked so hard to build a life worth capturing . . . but I wasn't present enough to live it.

In March 2009, all the units had sold, and my relationship with the developer ended naturally. I merged practices with my father and shifted focus to litigation and foreclosure work. The market was turning, but I had proven myself. I had made it.

Or so I thought.

Success without alignment is like a house built on sand. It may look impressive from the outside, but it cannot withstand the inevitable storms of life.

The images of success that surrounded me were clear and compelling: the prestigious credentials, the thriving practice, the beautiful family, the respected position in the community. These were the markers of achievement I had been chasing since childhood, the proof points that my parents' sacrifice had been worthwhile, that I had fulfilled the unspoken contract of the immigrant child.

But I had carefully constructed the perfect frame, prestigious education, thriving legal practice, beautiful family, respected community position, without truly living within it. I was so busy perfecting the appearance of my life that I missed the substance of living it. The frame gleamed with polish and promise, but the picture inside was becoming increasingly hollow. I was performing for the frame rather than being present in my life.

The subtle ways we justify our choices, the small compromises we make in service of success, the gradual erosion of our own ethical boundaries, these are not topics covered in law school. They don't show up in business plans or profit-and-loss statements. But they shape our destinies more surely than any strategic decision.

I had achieved everything I was supposed to achieve. I had checked every box, climbed every ladder, broken through every ceiling. I was the immigrant success story, the professional woman having it all, the perfect example of the American Dream.

But sitting in my modest office, surrounded by the trappings of success, I didn't feel the satisfaction I had expected. Something was missing, an emptiness I couldn't quite name, a quiet voice I had learned too well to ignore.

In my pursuit of the illusion of success, I had lost sight of what truly mattered. I had compromised my values, neglected my relationships, and ignored my intuition. The price of this misalignment was far higher than I could have imagined.

The true cost of success isn't measured in hours worked or sacrifices made. It's measured in the subtle compromises we make with ourselves, the small silences where our integrity used to speak.

Two years later, the FBI would walk into my office. And I would have time to examine every decision, every justification, every moment when I could have chosen differently. But in the rush of success, in the intoxication of achievement, those moments didn't feel like choices at all.

They felt like a necessity. Like opportunity. Like the natural next steps on the path I had been groomed to walk since childhood.

The perfect child had become the perfect professional and had achieved the perfect success. And in that perfection lay the seeds of my greatest failure, and eventually, my most profound transformation.

The illusion of success is a mirage that keeps moving as we approach it. The metrics keep changing, the goalposts keep shifting, the satisfaction remains elusive. **True success, I now understand, comes from alignment, when your actions reflect your values, when your achievements serve your purpose, and when your external reality matches your internal truth.**

This isn't about rejecting ambition or achievement. It's about anchoring that ambition in something deeper than approval, status, or material gain. It's about defining success on your own terms rather than accepting the definitions handed to you by family, culture, or society.

For business leaders, this lesson is particularly vital. Companies built on misalignment, where stated values contradict operational realities, where mission statements are divorced from daily decisions, where short-term profits consistently trump long-term purpose, are built on unstable foundations. They may achieve temporary success, but they rarely create lasting impact.

True success comes not from what you achieve but from who you become in the process. Not from what you accumulate but from what you create. Not from how you appear but from how you impact.

The journey from illusory success to authentic achievement begins with a simple question: What truly matters to me? Not to my parents, my peers, my community, my industry, but to me.

What would success look like if I were the only one defining it?

When we align our actions with our answers to these questions, we create not just better lives but better organizations, better communities, and better worlds. We trade the illusion of success for the reality of contribution.

And that, I've learned, is a trade worth making.

LEADERSHIP LESSONS: THE ILLUSION OF SUCCESS IS A TRAP

1. **Success without alignment is empty.** Titles, clients, and revenue may look like wins, but if they aren't rooted in your true values, they become traps rather than triumphs. Regular reflection on whether your

definition of success aligns with your deeper values is essential for sustainable achievement.

2. **Beware the cost of proving.** When your drive comes from needing to prove yourself, it clouds judgment and opens the door to ethical compromise or burnout. Notice when you're making decisions to impress others rather than to express your values.
3. **Misalignment masks as opportunity.** Leaders must build the muscle to pause and question red flags, even when they come wrapped in a big paycheck. The most dangerous temptations come disguised as exactly what we've been searching for.
4. **Presence is the rarest currency.** Building a business or career "for your family" means nothing if you're never truly with them. Success that costs your presence in your own life is failure disguised as achievement.

REFLECTION QUESTIONS

- What are the external markers of success that you're currently pursuing? How do these align with your deeper values and what truly matters to you?
- If you could redefine success on your own terms, free from others' expectations, what would that look like? How would your priorities and decisions change?
- What's one small step you could take today to bring your actions into greater alignment with your authentic values?

CHAPTER 3

When Everything Falls Apart

The morning the FBI walked into my office began like any other. It was May 2011: sunlight streaming through the windows, the hum of printers and phones, the familiar rhythm of a successful law practice in motion. I was reviewing case files when my receptionist appeared at my door, her face carrying an expression I'd never seen before.

"There are two FBI agents here to see you."

Time seemed to slow, then stop completely. In that suspended moment between her words and my response, a thousand thoughts raced through my mind. But the loudest was my own voice, confident and clear: "I have nothing to hide."

It's strange how we can lie to ourselves so convincingly.

"Show them in," I heard myself say, my voice steady despite the sudden racing of my heart. Two agents entered my office, a man and a woman, both carrying folders thick with documents. They showed me their badges and asked if they could sit down.

For the next four hours, I answered their questions without an attorney present. It never occurred to me to call one. I was a lawyer myself, after all. I understood the law. I was one of the good ones.

They showed me emails, documents, photographs. Asked me about closings from years ago, about conversations I barely remembered. Each time, I gave them absolute answers, definitive statements. No maybes, no "I don't recall." I was still performing perfection, still trying to be the A+ student, even as the ground was crumbling beneath me.

When the FBI agents showed me their badges, the frame I had spent my entire life constructing began to crack. Each document they placed before me, each question they asked, widened the fissures in the perfect picture I had created. By the time they left with the subpoena, I was staring at a shattered frame that could no longer contain the illusion I had been maintaining. The perfect picture was broken, forcing me to confront what lay beneath the carefully curated image I had presented to the world.

CRISIS REVEALS LEADERSHIP CHARACTER

Crisis is a leadership crucible. Your most defining moments won't come from success but from how you lead when everything unravels. When the FBI walked into my office that day, I made an immediate decision that would shape everything that followed: I chose performance over protection, certainty over caution. Leaders face similar moments daily, perhaps less dramatic but no less defining. Do you speak with false confidence when unsure? Do you bypass necessary counsel in your rush to appear in control? These are the crucible moments that reveal your leadership foundation.

At some point during the interview, I called my father in. He sat quietly beside me, his presence both comforting and concerning. Here was the man who had taught me about integrity, watching as federal agents questioned his daughter's actions.

When they finally left, handing me a subpoena for documents, my father turned to me with tears in his eyes. "Honey," he said softly, "what happened?"

I wish I had been able to answer him honestly then. I wish I had been able to say, "I got lost in the pursuit of success. I stopped asking hard questions because I was afraid of the answers. I chose not to see what I didn't want to see."

Instead, I said what I had been telling myself: "Nothing happened, Dad. This is just a misunderstanding." I went home and told Erik. That evening we even had dinner with Kendall Coffey, a mentor and friend as well as the former US attorney for the Southern District of Florida. We briefed him because he insisted; I certainly would not have known better.

After the FBI left that day, life took on a surreal quality. On the surface, everything continued as normal. I met with clients, reviewed contracts, and attended community events. But internally, a constant hum of anxiety accompanied every moment.

I threw myself into preparing the subpoenaed documents, approaching the task with the same perfectionism that had defined my entire life. Every file was meticulously organized, every document carefully labeled. Even in potential legal jeopardy, I was still trying to be the perfect student turning in the perfect assignment.

But I also tried to fix things. When I examined the files that had been uploaded to a scanning company, I noticed that my staff failed to include notes on wire transfers and other documents as I thought they would have done. In my gut, I already knew. Something was wrong. So I tried to alter the documents and have them reuploaded. This attempt to "cover up" or "fix" the past to make it all look alright only further contributed to the problem that was about to overcome my life.

The strain of the investigation wasn't just legal; it was deeply personal. In 2012, Erik and I separated. The weight of the ongoing federal inquiry, combined with years of my absence even when physically present, had taken its toll on our marriage. We hadn't learned how to properly communicate through our challenges.

I was still chasing achievements, still measuring my worth through external validation, still unable to let go of the perfectionist drive that had defined me since childhood. I hadn't yet learned how to simply be present, how to value connection over accomplishment. Erik was dealing with his own struggles, and neither of us had developed the tools to navigate our difficulties together.

The separation felt like another failure to add to my growing list, another way I was disappointing the people who mattered most. Even as my professional world was crumbling under federal scrutiny, I couldn't stop performing, couldn't stop trying to be perfect, couldn't figure out how to just be real with the people who loved me most.

Two years passed. The investigation seemed to fade into the background, becoming just another worry I carried but didn't discuss. Our practice was growing. I was focused on building the litigation department, targeting big banks for their Florida foreclosure cases. Life moved forward.

Then, in June 2013, another grand jury subpoena arrived. This time, it was delivered to Kendall Coffey, the former US attorney who had become my mentor and friend. The moment I saw his name flash on my phone, something in me knew, this was the beginning of the end.

"They're not just looking for documents this time, Rashmi," Kendall said gently. "They're building a case."

THE FALL STRIPS AWAY THE FALSE

When your title, reputation, and identity collapse, what's left is the raw material of authentic leadership. For years, I had been hiding behind the ideal image of a successful attorney and community leader. The investigation was stripping that away, layer by painful layer. Organizations go through similar processes during crises, whether it's a public scandal, a failed product launch, or a financial downturn. What's left when the glossy exterior is stripped away? Is there a core of integrity, values, and authenticity? Or just more facade?

I remember sitting in Kendall's office weeks later, the Miami sunlight harsh against the windows, as he explained what the evidence suggested. The prosecutor, Joe Capone, had been trying to get me to come in and talk. "He keeps saying you still have time," Kendall explained. "Maybe they'll cut you a deal."

But I was still clinging to my carefully constructed reality. "I don't know anything," I insisted. "What am I supposed to tell them?"

The truth, I now realize, is that I didn't want to know. I had built such elaborate justifications for my actions that acknowledging the truth would mean dismantling my entire understanding of who I was.

One Tuesday evening in February 2014, I was at the temple with my parents and my best friend, Shanti. We were doing Hanuman

Puja, chanting prayers to the monkey god known for his strength and devotion. My phone buzzed; it was Kendall calling again.

I stepped outside the main prayer room to take the call. "Joe is going to indict," he said simply. "Within two weeks."

I collapsed against the cold white cement wall, my back scraping as I slid down until the floor caught me. My legs refused to hold me, as if the strength I had carried for so long had finally abandoned me. The trembling that had stalked me in moments of stress now consumed me, waves of uncontrollable shaking coursing through every muscle. My chest tightened, each breath shallow, as if even oxygen were slipping beyond my reach.

Shanti found me crumpled there, my body folded into grief and panic I could not contain. She knelt beside me, her hand wrapping around mine, an anchor in a storm I could not steady. I clung to her touch, trying to draw air into lungs that felt clamped shut, willing myself not to drown in the terror that pressed down on me.

The indictment came in April 2014. One count of conspiracy to commit bank fraud and twenty-four counts of bank fraud. The words were clinical, but they sliced me open. The numbers were absurd, almost unrecognizable, like they belonged to someone else's nightmare. I stared at them and could not reconcile how I, the perfect student, the community leader, the devoted mother, had been reduced in an instant to this: a criminal defendant. The titles I had worn with pride felt ripped away, replaced with one that burned with shame.

The day the grand jury indictment was unsealed, my private nightmare became public reality. I had known this moment was coming since Kendall's call at the temple, but nothing could have prepared me for the stark brutality of the federal criminal justice system in action.

The federal courthouse in Fort Lauderdale felt like a fortress that morning. The weight of what was about to unfold pressed down on me like a physical force. This wasn't just another legal proceeding; this was the moment I would officially become a criminal defendant in the eyes of the law.

My support system gathered around me with a loyalty so fierce it brought me to tears. My parents sat in the front row, their faces etched with deep worry, yet beneath the lines of fear was a love so steady it seemed to wrap itself around me like armor. My dad's eyes carried both anguish and pride, and my mom's hands were clasped tightly in her lap, as if she were holding all of us together by sheer force of will.

Erik was there too, even with all that had broken between us. Whatever had fractured in our marriage, he understood that this moment was larger than us, larger than any personal struggle. For that day, he showed up, and his presence mattered.

Meredith had flown in from Richmond the night before, leaving her own life behind without hesitation. She has always been the kind of friend who doesn't wait for an invitation, who simply arrives when you need her most. Seeing her there reminded me that real friendship is not measured in years but in the willingness to step into someone else's storm.

And then there was Taimy, my guardian angel, my adopted sister, who had worked beside me for years. She did not need to say anything. Her quiet strength filled the space between us, reminding me that sometimes presence alone is the greatest comfort. Her calm was like a steady heartbeat, keeping me from falling apart completely.

I looked at them and felt both crushed by the shame of dragging them into this nightmare and lifted by the fierce love that refused to let me face it alone.

David Markus met us at the courthouse entrance after security. His face was grim as he pulled me aside for a brief conversation before we entered the courtroom.

"Rashmi, I need to tell you something," he said, his voice low and serious. "Your case has been assigned to Judge William Zloch." I could tell from his expression that this wasn't good news, though I didn't fully understand the implications yet. "It's not good news," he continued, confirming my instinct. "But we'll make the best of it and figure out what to do."

That simple statement, "We'll make the best of it," would become a theme of our attorney-client relationship. David never sugarcoated reality, but he also never abandoned hope. His honesty about the challenges ahead, combined with his commitment to fighting for me regardless, gave me a foundation of trust that would prove crucial in the months to come.

When they called my case, "United States of America v. Rashmi Airan-Pace," the formal weight of those words hit me. This wasn't a civil dispute or a contract negotiation. This was the full power of the federal government aligned against me, one person.

I first laid eyes on Joe Capone as he stood at the prosecution table. In that moment, I hated him. Here was the man who had spent months building a case against me, who had dissected my life and found me wanting, who now stood ready to argue for my imprisonment. He looked younger than I had expected, but there was a steely determination in his demeanor that made it clear he took his role seriously.

The magistrate judge presided over the arraignment with clinical efficiency. The charges were read aloud: conspiracy to commit bank fraud, twenty-four counts of bank fraud. The numbers felt abstract and surreal. How had my life become reduced to these cold legal terms?

"How do you plead?" the magistrate asked.

"Not guilty, Your Honor," I replied, my voice steadier than I felt.

The discussion turned to bond conditions. David had worked with Joe to prenegotiate the terms, a signature bond that would require both my signature and Erik's, acknowledging our joint responsibility for ensuring I would appear for all future court proceedings.

"The defendant will be released on a signature bond in the amount previously agreed upon by the parties," the magistrate announced. "The conditions of release include surrendering your passport, remaining within the Southern District of Florida without court permission, and reporting to pretrial services as directed."

Each condition was another bar in an invisible cage that was closing around me. My freedom, which I had taken for granted for forty-three years, was now entirely conditional. But then came the moment that will forever be seared into my memory, and into the hearts of my family watching helplessly from the gallery.

"The defendant will be remanded to the custody of the US Marshals for processing before release," the magistrate announced.

I felt my legs go weak. Processing. That clinical word couldn't capture what it actually meant.

Two US Marshals approached me at the defense table. They were professional but firm, treating me not as the attorney I had been just moments before, but as what I now legally was, a criminal defendant in federal custody.

"Please turn around and put your hands behind your back," one of them said quietly.

The cold bite of metal closed around my wrists, the handcuffs locking into place with a sharp click that echoed louder than any gavel. The sound seemed to reverberate through my chest, sealing a reality I could hardly absorb. Behind me I heard my mother's gasp, quick and sharp, a sound that pierced deeper than the cuffs themselves.

Then came the shackles, heavy iron gripping my ankles, a chain binding them together so tightly that even the smallest steps became clumsy and humiliating. A chain was fastened around my waist, connecting everything, forcing me into movements that were slow, deliberate, stripped of dignity. Every clink of metal announced to the courtroom that I was no longer free.

As the marshal led me toward the side door reserved for defendants being taken into custody, I forced myself to lift my eyes. I wanted, needed, one last look at the people who had carried me this far.

My dad's face was etched in agony, a man who had raised me on dignity and integrity now watching his eldest daughter reduced to chains. His eyes spoke what his lips could not: disbelief, grief, and love all tangled together.

Erik sat frozen, his expression blank with shock, as if he too could not reconcile the woman he married with the defendant before him. He knew his signature would soon be needed to secure my release, and yet his eyes betrayed how unprepared he was for this moment.

Meredith's tears fell freely, her whole body trembling as though she was trying to cry enough for both of us. She was breaking with me, and I felt it even from across the room.

And then there was Taimy, hands clasped tight, lips moving in silent prayer. Her strength radiated across the courtroom, a reminder that even in my chains, I was not abandoned.

I shuffled forward, every clank of the restraints pressing humiliation deeper into my skin. I had been stripped not only of freedom, but of the illusion that my achievements could protect me. All that was left was the searing gaze of the people I loved most, watching me disappear behind that door.

David watched with professional composure, but I could see the concern in his eyes. He had prepared me for this processing step, but witnessing it was different from discussing it in theory.

The door closed behind me with a finality that seemed to separate not just spaces but entire worlds. On one side was the courtroom where I had just been a person with constitutional rights and presumed innocence. On the other side was the federal detention system, where I was now simply a number to be processed.

The processing room was sterile and institutional, all concrete floors, fluorescent lighting, and metal furniture bolted to the ground. A federal officer directed me to a chair and began the methodical work of turning Rashmi Airan into an entry in the federal criminal database.

"Press each finger firmly on the scanner," he instructed, rolling my fingerprints with practiced efficiency. Each print was another piece of evidence that this was really happening, that I was really here.

The cheek swab for DNA came next. "Open your mouth," he said, running the cotton swab along the inside of my cheek. My genetic material would now be stored in federal databases alongside those of murderers, drug dealers, and terrorists.

Finally, they led me to a holding cell to wait for my release processing to be completed. The cell was small, maybe eight feet by six feet, with concrete walls painted an institutional green and metal bars that left no doubt about where I was.

I sat on the cold metal bench, and the full weight of my circumstances came crashing down with a force that nearly stole my breath. The cuffs had been removed, yet the ghost of them lingered, an ache pressing into my wrists as though the steel had branded itself into my skin. My ankles still bore the memory of the shackles, every nerve humming with the humiliation of having been bound.

The hallway was alive with sounds that made me feel even smaller. The shuffle of other defendants being processed. Voices calling out names. The metallic slam of doors locking behind them. The relentless buzz of fluorescent lights overhead, casting everything in a sterile glow that made time feel suspended. Each sound echoed through the hollow chambers of my chest until it felt like the building itself was mocking me.

For the first time since this nightmare began, I was truly alone with my thoughts. No family to reassure me. No lawyer to argue for me. Just me and the crushing silence between the noises.

And in that silence, my mind reached for my grandfather, my dadaji. I pictured him in a British prison cell in 1946, his body weakened from disease and confinement, yet his spirit unbroken. He had been imprisoned for his principles, for standing for justice and independence. I was here because I had betrayed mine. The shame of that truth seared through me.

Yet, strangely, there was comfort in the connection. Across time and space, our stories were bound by chains. He had endured suffering I could hardly imagine and had walked out stronger, his pain transformed into purpose. If he could hold his dignity in the face of injustice, then perhaps I could find a way to hold mine in the face of my failure.

I closed my eyes, tears sliding hot down my cheeks, and whispered a prayer. Not for escape, not for rescue from the consequences I had earned, but for strength. Strength to face what came next with integrity. Wisdom to find meaning in the wreckage. Courage to become a mother my children could one day respect again.

In that moment, the bench beneath me became more than metal. It became an altar. And my whispered prayer was a vow that I would not waste the pain.

After what felt like hours but was probably only forty-five minutes, the officer returned. "Your release paperwork is ready," he said, unlocking the cell door.

Walking back through that courthouse, past the security checkpoints and metal detectors, I felt fundamentally changed. I was technically free, released on bond to await trial, but I understood now that my old life was over. The woman who had walked into that courtroom that morning in a tailored suitdress, confident in her identity as a successful attorney, no longer existed.

In her place was someone I didn't yet know, someone who would have to figure out how to rebuild from the ground up, someone who would have to find meaning in the wreckage of everything she had thought defined her.

My family waited for me in the courthouse lobby, their faces a mixture of relief and continued worry. As we walked to the parking garage together, I realized that this was just the beginning. The arraignment was over, but the real work, the work of trying to prove that I was not guilty, consumed me.

About two weeks later, our house was filled with the Indian community who had been part of my life since childhood. The aunties who had fed me with their own hands, who had whispered prayers over me during exams. The uncles who had cheered at every graduation, who had carried my children as though they were their own grandchildren. These were the people who had celebrated every bright moment of my life. And now they had come to sit in the shadow of my darkest one.

My father stood in the corner of the living room, his shoulders slumped in a way I had never seen before. Tears streamed down his face as he tried to find words. With a voice cracked open by grief, he told them about the indictment. The room felt unbearably heavy, as though even the air was holding its breath.

I braced myself for judgment. I expected the silence of disapproval, the averted eyes, the slow but certain distancing that shame often brings. I thought I would lose not only my reputation but also the community that had held me since birth.

Instead, one uncle leaned forward, his eyes steady on mine. In a voice both gentle and firm he said, "Beti, one day you will realize this is not happening to you. It is happening for you."

The words landed like a foreign language. I could not comprehend them, not then. My body was too consumed by shame, my heart too crushed under the weight of fear. Every thought was of my children. What would this mean for them, for their future, for the way the world would look at them because of me?

I could not yet understand his meaning, but his words planted a seed. A small one, almost invisible under the soil of my panic and disgrace. But it was there, waiting for the day when I would be able to water it with perspective, when I could let it grow into something that would eventually change how I saw everything.

RADICAL ACCOUNTABILITY TRANSFORMS CULTURE

In organizations, as in life, the willingness to see uncomfortable truths, without defensiveness, is the gateway to reinvention. My uncle's words contained a profound truth that would take me a while to fully understand: Transformation begins with radical acceptance. This applies to corporate culture as much as personal growth. When organizations create space for uncomfortable truths to be spoken, they create the foundation for genuine innovation and resilience.

The months that followed became a war room operation. I converted my parents' extra bedroom into a document review center. I printed out the entire discovery, 200,000 pages of documents and 15,000 emails. I was convinced I would find the smoking gun to prove my innocence.

Instead, I found something far more valuable: the truth.

Every day, I dropped the kids off at school or camp and returned to the war room to dig through the documents. I needed to save my ass. I needed to find the evidence that would exonerate me. I combed through every email and every page. But I kept finding bad documents. Ones that I knew would destroy me.

Every few weeks, I met with David, my new attorney, and his partner, Margot Moss, to go over what we'd found. We separated the documents into two piles. One pile that would help me and another pile that wouldn't.

In August 2014, David and Margot asked my parents and me to come in for a meeting. The trial was set for December. We walked into their small conference room thinking we were going to discuss trial preparation strategy, exhibits, and expert witnesses. Instead, David and Margot presented how things would pan out for me if I decided to go to trial.

"Rashmi, this is what you are charged with, and here is the evidence the government will use to prove their case," Margot began, her tone steady and deliberate. Page after page unfolded across the table, each document like a stone being stacked on my chest. "And this will be our defense and the evidence we will use to support our arguments."

I shuddered, my body instinctively recoiling even as I sat motionless. My hands went cold. My breath turned shallow. It was as if my skin itself were trying to retreat from the reality being laid bare. Then came the next blow. "And this is what the government will use for their rebuttal."

The room seemed to tighten around me, every sound amplified: the shuffle of paper, the click of Margot's pen, the faint hum of the air conditioning. I felt myself slipping into numbness, as though detachment was the only way to survive hearing how the world now defined me.

Through the fog, I glanced at David. He had not spoken a word. His jaw was tight, but his eyes gave him away. They were wet with tears. Silent, unguarded tears.

It startled me. Why was he the one crying while I sat frozen, unable to release anything? His tears carried a message I had not yet grasped: This was not just a legal strategy session. This was the fire that would burn away everything I thought I was, the crucible where something new could be forged.

Purpose can be born in the fire. Rock bottom can become the place where vision takes root if you dare to look inward. David's tears told me the magnitude of what was happening before I could see it myself. They revealed what I did not yet understand. This moment would not only change my case, but it would also change the direction of my entire life.

I did not get it then. Not fully. I was still too stunned, too scared, too numb. And then David spoke.

"Rashmi, you are our client. If you ask us to go to trial, we will. We will fight and do the best we can. But I'm telling you right now that you will lose. Look, I've known you a long time. I know you didn't go into this planning and trying to commit a crime. But you knew enough. You could have asked more questions. And as a lawyer, you had a fiduciary duty to dig deeper. And here is the thing: You did know. Right? You knew there was a rental guarantee and that the buyers were getting a financial benefit, which is not legal. If and when you lose, you are facing twenty years in prison. Rashmi, you will miss it all. Your kids' whole lives."

David understood both the finality of the decision and the enormity of how this choice would affect my family and me. During the meeting, my dad was so overcome with emotion that he had to walk out of the conference room six separate times, each return more fragile than the last. I sat at the table quivering, my skin clammy, my breath shallow, as though my body itself were rejecting the reality settling over us. It was one of the hardest days of my life. Questions tumbled through my mind faster than I could speak them, and every answer seemed to close another door.

When I glanced at David, I saw tears escaping the corners of his eyes. He was not simply a lawyer in that moment. He was a witness to my breaking, to the unbearable weight pressing down on all of us. His tears told me he felt the depth of my pain.

We all sat in tears, except for my mom. She held herself steady, her face hard as stone, the way she always had when life demanded survival. But the rest of us broke openly. And in that breaking, something shifted inside me.

I finally understood. I was being indicted not because I had acted, but because I had not. Because I turned my back on what was happening in front of me. Because I failed to ask the questions that mattered. Because silence, too, is a choice. Not doing something is still doing something wrong.

In that moment, I decided to own my mistake. It was the first time I let the truth settle into my bones. And with that truth came another realization that hollowed me out completely: I was going to be a convicted felon for the rest of my life.

This was failure. All the achievements I had worked so hard to attain, everything I did to make my parents and entire Indian community proud, were lost. It felt like an out-of-body experience where I was looking down at my life, unsure how I would survive the next stage.

The decision to plead guilty wasn't just about legal strategy; it was about finally being honest with myself. I had known enough to ask questions. I had chosen not to. I had seen red flags and looked away. I had allowed my drive for success to override my ethical compass.

The morning of December 19, 2014, I woke with a knot in my stomach that had been growing tighter for weeks. This wasn't just another court appearance; this was the day I would officially become a criminal defendant and stand before a federal judge to admit my guilt.

David had prepared me for what would happen and walked me through each step of the process. But no amount of preparation could ready me for the emotional weight of that moment, or the stakes involved. If Judge Darrin Gayles didn't accept my plea, if he thought I wasn't being completely honest, I was looking at twenty years in prison.

The federal courthouse felt different this time. The marble floors that had once seemed impressive now felt cold and unforgiving.

Inside the courtroom, Judge Gayles presided with the solemn gravity that marked every movement, every word. The room itself seemed designed to remind me of the seriousness of what was unfolding. Wood-paneled walls stretched high above me, polished and imposing, while the American flag stood tall at the judge's bench, a silent witness to justice and judgment alike.

At the prosecution table sat Joe Capone and his team, their files stacked in meticulous order, each page ready to be used against me. The air carried a sharp stillness, broken only by the soft shuffle of papers and the occasional squeak of a chair. Every detail of the room pressed down on me, amplifying the reality that my life as I knew it was about to end.

When my name was called, my legs trembled so violently it felt as though the floor itself might give way beneath me. Still, I forced myself forward, each step heavy and unsteady, the sound of my heels echoing like a drumbeat of finality. I reached the podium, my throat tight, my body pulsing with fear.

David stood beside me, his presence steady, his silence carrying both reassurance and a sobering reminder. This was no rehearsal, no theoretical exercise. This was real. My plea, my shame, and my truth were about to be spoken out loud. And in that instant, the weight of it all nearly brought me to my knees.

Judge Gayles looked down at me with serious eyes. "Ms. Airan-Pace, you are here today to enter a plea of guilty to the charges against you. Before I can accept your plea, I need to ensure you understand what you are doing."

What followed was a methodical series of questions designed to ensure my plea was knowing and voluntary. Each question felt like a small death of my former identity.

"Do you understand the charges against you?"

"Yes, Your Honor."

"Do you understand that by pleading guilty, you are giving up your right to vote?"

My knees began to shake. David, sensing my distress, placed his hand gently on my back to steady me. I had voted in every election since I was eighteen years old. I took that civic privilege seriously; it was part of my identity as an engaged citizen, as someone who believed in participating in democracy.

"Yes, Your Honor," I managed to say, though my voice wavered.

"Do you understand you are giving up your right to serve on a jury?"

Another fundamental right, another piece of citizenship stripped away. The weight of what I was surrendering began to sink in fully.

"Yes, Your Honor."

The questions continued, each one requiring me to acknowledge another consequence of my choices. Judge Gayles was thorough and methodical and ensured that I understood the full scope of what I was admitting to.

"Are you pleading guilty because you are, in fact, guilty?"

I paused. This was the moment of truth, not just legally but personally. For months I had been constructing elaborate explanations, finding ways to minimize my culpability. But standing there, with my family watching, with the weight of twenty years hanging over me if the judge didn't accept my plea, there was only one honest answer.

"Yes, Your Honor."

The hearing was quick, but every moment felt meaningful. I knew I had to hold myself completely accountable, had to be absolutely real and honest. Judge Gayles was watching me carefully, assessing whether my remorse was genuine, whether I truly understood what I had done.

Finally, after what felt like an eternity but was probably only minutes, Judge Gayles spoke: "I accept your plea of guilty."

With those words, I officially became a convicted felon. The gavel came down, but instead of feeling defeated, I felt something unexpected, a strange kind of freedom. The pretense was over. The performance had ended. Now I could begin the work of becoming who I was meant to be.

As we left the courtroom, I realized that my fall from grace was now official. But walking with David, supported by David's steadying hand when my knees gave way, I no longer felt the desperate need to manage my image. The worst had happened, and I was still standing.

That night, I sat across from Kyler at The Cheesecake Factory. He was only ten years old, his feet long and quietly resting on the floor beneath the table, his face still holding the softness of childhood. He had just finished reading John Grisham's kids' series about law and justice, a book filled with heroes and clear lines between right and wrong. I wondered how he would see me now.

"Kyler," I began, my voice trembling, "today Mommy had to plead guilty to a crime in federal court. I had to admit it to myself and then to everyone else. But most importantly, I want you and your sister to be proud of me."

He looked at me with wide eyes, sadness spilling into them, and said, "But Mommy, I will always be proud of you. But do you think you're going to have to go away?"

The words pierced me. He was so much like me, already trying to carry more than he should, already stepping into the role of the strong oldest child. I could see the conflict on his little face: wanting to protect me, yet terrified of what my answer might be.

"I don't know, honey," I whispered, my throat tightening. "We'll find out at my sentencing hearing."

The dam broke. We both cried, our bodies shaking, tears falling into the plates in front of us. It was gut-wrenching to see my child carry a weight no child should ever have to bear. It was humbling to realize how deeply my choices had scarred not just me but him. And it was life-changing, because in his innocent, unconditional love, Kyler taught me something that night that no courtroom ever could.

The leadership crucible reveals character. Difficult moments do not just shape character; they expose it. My son's response, his loyalty and love in the face of my confession, revealed more integrity than I had shown in my business dealings. He loved me without conditions, without hesitation, without calculation. That was true character.

In business, we face similar crucibles: when a product fails, when we make a serious mistake, when we must deliver devastating news. These moments strip away the façade and reveal what we are really made of. They show whether our leadership is built on image or integrity.

The months between my decision to plead guilty and my sentencing became a time of profound transformation. I began to understand what my uncle meant about this happening for me, not to me. Each painful revelation, each moment of accountability, was stripping away layers of perfectionism and performance that had imprisoned me for decades.

I made a spreadsheet of everyone in my life: friends from elementary school through college, law school colleagues, community members, my children's teachers and their friends' parents. One by one, I called each person to tell them the truth about my case.

I expected rejection. Instead, I found grace. Person after person responded not with judgment but with love. They shared their own struggles, their own failures, their own journeys of redemption.

After I pled guilty, I made a very conscious decision to be transparent. All I could think was how I had disgraced my family, my community, my friends, and more. I had let everybody down. Every teacher who believed in me. Every boss who'd taught me. Every group I'd given my time to in the community. I didn't know if people would love me after they learned what I'd done.

I needed to personally tell the people in my life. I didn't want them to read about it in the paper. I had no idea if the US Attorney's Office was going to issue a press release. But I knew I didn't want people to read about me.

I thought every person would shun me. I had convinced myself that my friends, mentors, and colleagues respected me because of my accomplishments and professional acumen. I was prepared for people to hang up on me or disparage me. They didn't.

Authenticity transforms connection. In a business world obsessed with perfection, authenticity becomes your greatest differentiator. Organizations that foster cultures where failure can be discussed openly don't just prevent bigger issues; they build unprecedented loyalty and innovation. When people can bring their whole selves to work, including their struggles, creativity and engagement flourish. My vulnerable calls to share my failure created deeper connections than did all my years of professional success.

I started to make my calls. I gave details. Rather than point fingers and deflect, I took accountability for what happened and why I ended up getting indicted. I went into specifics and chronology. The calls were emotional and took a toll. Between the tears and conversations, I was only able to muster the strength to complete five to six calls a day.

What occurred was unimaginable and surprising. Each person said they would support me unconditionally, debunking my theory that I had been loved for my perceived perfection and for what I had attained in life. At the end of each call, I asked each person if they would feel comfortable writing a letter of support to the judge and sharing stories about me. David said the letters would give Judge Gayles a glimpse of me as a human being. As the weeks passed, David and I began to receive letters.

While I had encouraged each person to write from their heart and to tell specific experiences they remembered having with me, I never could have predicted the words written about me. It's like I was eulogized before I died.

Patrick, an old friend from junior high school, wrote, "I do not know how I would have made it through those years without the countless hours on the phone and in person sharing my experiences with Rashmi and seeking her thoughtful and patient guidance and support. She gave me as much time as I needed, and she undoubtedly put aside her own interests to help me."

My dear friend, Amisha, whom I met in my adult years, said, "Rashmi is a unique individual that truly is selfless. She puts others before herself and has boundless compassion. She has reminded me to always look for the true goodness in people, to be less cynical and eternally grateful. She lives her life as she preaches, and those around her reap the benefits."

One hundred eighty-two friends, family members, colleagues, and mentors took time to express how I had impacted them. The outpouring of support with thoughtful and elaborate details about my character was overwhelming. I had spent most of my life worried about fitting in and whether people really liked me. And yet here were almost two hundred people actively helping me because they believed in me without question.

I was unbelievably touched and moved to tears. It was like peering out from under a heavy wool blanket that I had kept myself under my whole life with a story I told myself.

The judge ultimately got a binder of letters an inch and a half thick prior to the sentencing hearing, a copy of which sits on my nightstand still.

On the day of my sentencing, I breathed heavy and wiped the sweat off my face from my long run. I tiptoed through the front door back into the house. Today was the day Judge Gayles would decide if I would be taken away from my kids. The kids were still sleeping, and I wanted to shower before waking them. Steam surrounded me as my phone alarm rang. I needed to get the kids up and ready. I couldn't be late. They ate and dressed quickly, and I drove them to camp.

"Today is going to be . . . ?" I asked my daily question before they got out of the car.

"An awesome day!" we yelled.

My family caravan entered the parking garage and walked toward 400 North Miami Avenue. Summer had arrived, and I second-guessed the suit I was wearing because I was already starting to sweat. As I approached the federal courthouse, I noticed a line coming out of the security area around the building. At first, I was confused.

Why are there so many people here? Oh no, I'm going to be late for my own sentencing hearing. And then I realized the line was for me. All these people were waiting to go through security to attend *my* sentencing hearing.

The fall reveals your foundation. When everything is stripped away—title, status, professional identity—what remains is your true foundation. On my sentencing day, I discovered that my foundation wasn't my achievements but the relationships I'd built. The line of people waiting to support me revealed what truly mattered.

David had told me it would help if I had support in the courtroom, so I sent an email to everyone that had written a letter. I hoped a few people would come. School was already out, and I figured people would be out of town or in summer mode and wouldn't show up. I was wrong.

Standing in the attorney's small room outside the courtroom designated for the defense, David and Margot reminded me what would happen in the hearing. I had prepared my allocution. I would apologize to everyone, especially my family and community. Tears welled up in my eyes as the knots in my stomach were a clear reminder of the enormity of the day. I steeled myself.

And then Joe walked into our room. *Why is the prosecutor walking into the defense room?* David looked at me with a confused look.

"Rashmi, I know you will get through this. Stay strong." And with that, Joe leaned in, gave me a huge bear hug, and walked out.

David said, "In all my years of being a criminal defense lawyer, I have never had a prosecutor walk in and hug my client. Ever. It's such a testament to you, Rashmi." I had no idea how unusual it was. For the past few months, David and Mona, his wife and law partner, along with Margot, their partner, kept reminding me how unusual it was to receive not only the quantity of letters but the quality of comments and stories about me. Mona had prepared the sentencing memorandum for the judge and quoted many of the letters. Mona said, "This memo is so powerful not because of my writing but because of the substance of what people wrote about you and how much they believe in you."

I was still coming to a place in my heart where I allowed myself the freedom to feel loved and respected by others. David and Mona were well known in the criminal defense field and had represented high-profile defendants. It was hard for me to believe I was unique. But Mona had told me several times that, in fact, the sentencing memorandum filed on my behalf was exceptional mostly because people valued me.

How crazy. I've tried my whole life to get people to like me and was never really sure they did. But maybe, just maybe, I was focused on the wrong metrics.

My heels wobbled as I entered the courtroom. Smiles, kind eyes, and head nods surrounded me on both sides of the aisle. David pushed open the swinging barrier between the attorneys' tables and the viewers. I slid the chair back between David and Margot and sat down.

One by one, friends kept filing into the visitor pews. They scrunched together. I had held back tears all morning, but when Dana and Jen walked in, I erupted. I had no idea they were coming. I found out later in the evening that Dana, a dear friend from UNC, left Charlotte at 11:00 the night before to drive to Miami to be here for me. As soon as the hearing was done, he got in his car and drove back. Jen, my college roommate and a doctor in NYC, flew down that morning and then flew back in the evening.

Rock bottom isn't the end; it becomes your foundation.

What feels like an ending can become the beginning of something more meaningful than you ever imagined. In the moment of my sentencing, surrounded by people who loved me despite my failures, I began to understand that this painful experience could become the foundation for something new.

Organizations that survive crisis often emerge stronger precisely because they've been forced to build on a more authentic foundation. The companies that transform failure into fuel for reinvention don't just recover; they redefine their industries.

By the time the hearing started, it was standing room only. The courtroom security had to ask people to stand in the waiting area. The outpouring of love was more than I could have ever expected.

"All rise. The Honorable Judge Darrin Gayles." The clerk announced the judge's entrance as my community stood in respect for the man who would decide my fate. I really didn't know what the judge would do. Joe made his way to the podium. He told the judge that I had taken responsibility for my actions. "Rashmi has gone above and beyond what I asked of her. She has cooperated with the prosecution and helped in ways that we had not expected her to do." Joe then asked for a downward departure from the federal sentencing guidelines due to my cooperation with the investigation, known as a Rule 5K1.

I had only learned what this was while preparing for the hearing with David. Once Joe uttered the magical combination of numbers and letters, Judge Gayles had the legal authority and discretion to go below the guidelines. I knew this was important.

It was now David's turn in the hearing. He was prepared and smart, just as I knew he would be. He didn't let his voice shake, and he got through his presentation. As he sat down, the TVs came on. My sentencing video began to play.

Billy Corben, a highly respected documentary director, had created a powerful video featuring testimonials from people who knew me. The courtroom grew silent as judges, mentors, friends, and community members spoke about my character, my contributions, and the person they believed I truly was.

When the video ended, I pushed my chair back, stood up, and carefully made my way to the podium. The carpet softened the sound of my heels as I took each step. The podium was located dead center in the courtroom. My eyes saw wood. Wood walls around me, wood desks next to me, a wood podium, and an empty wood jury box. I looked straight at Judge Gayles. He was seated higher than everyone else in the courtroom. The reading glasses he used to watch the video were now in his hands.

I knew this would be hard. I didn't even know what an allocution was a few months ago. David explained that it was my time to apologize and say any last words before the judge sentenced me. I tried looking it up, but that wasn't helpful. So I sat down a week before and wrote from my heart.

"Your Honor, thank you for the opportunity to address the Court. I would like to first apologize for my unlawful actions that have brought me before you. I was wrong, and I accept full responsibility for my conduct and its consequences. There is no excuse for what I did. I am deeply ashamed of violating the moral code by which I have strived to live and which I have sought to instill in others."

I looked at my parents and apologized for letting them down. More than anything, this pained me the most. In that moment I believed I had failed them.

Not able to hold back my tears, I stumbled through to the end of my written notes. I apologized to my community and promised to be better and to continue to give back. I turned and walked back to my seat. I didn't look at anyone, but I knew there was empathy and compassion around me. I could feel it. The energy was thick with love and grace.

It was in the hands of Judge Gayles. We had asked for home confinement. We argued that taking me away from Kyler and Maya would serve no benefit to the public and community and would only harm my children significantly. Since Joe had opened the door with his 5K1 motion, the judge could order whatever sentence he deemed appropriate. The lumps in my gut tightened. I smelled a rank odor and felt like I was going to throw up. Everything else faded away, and the entire courtroom felt empty as I stared at the judge and waited.

And then he pulled the microphone closer to his mouth and began. He said he recognized that I had helped the prosecution and had owned it by taking responsibility and admitting what I did wrong. He acknowledged house arrest as a sufficient penalty given that I had already lost my bar license and so much more financially. Judge Gayles then said he believed the defendant (me) had a fiduciary duty to ask more questions and that she (I) failed to do so. He then entered his order.

"I am sentencing Ms. Airan-Pace to one year and one day incarceration followed by three years' supervised release, two hundred hours of community service," and the payment of an amount approximately 150 times the income I had earned working with my client: $19 million in restitution. Now, nine years later, having served incarceration, three years' supervised release, and completed my community service hours, I am still paying off the $19 million month by month.

I collapsed on the ground and began to hysterically cry. I was shaking. Uncontrollably. The only thought in my head was, *What's going to happen to my kids?* The judge exited the courtroom, and David and Margot tried to console me. A sea of people enveloped me, but I couldn't see anyone. My mind was spinning, and my eyes went blurry. As I wobbled to my feet, Joe walked up and hugged me. He looked me straight in the eye and said, "You'll be fine. You can do this."

PURPOSE EMERGES FROM PAIN

What feels like destruction is often the beginning of something more authentic and meaningful. The sentence that seemed like the end of my world would become the catalyst for my greatest contribution. Leaders who navigate organizational crises most effectively are those who can see beyond the immediate pain to the possibility it contains. The question isn't "How do we get back to normal?" but "What new purpose might emerge from this challenge?"

David was standing on a bench outside the courtroom in the lobby area, poised to talk to my family and friends who had come. He was trying to comfort them. I sat next to his feet, cradling my wet cheeks.

This has to be a nightmare. This can't really be happening. What will happen to Kyler and Maya? How will I tell them?

Up until that moment, I had shouted out daily affirmations to the universe to protect me and to keep me with my children. I had faith. I trusted that whatever the outcome was, it would be "for" me. But did I really have complete faith? Or was I trapped in the privileged thinking that I was afforded the chance to even fathom? Sure, I knew that the plea deal carried a five-year maximum sentence and that our request for house arrest was a stretch. But I really thought the judge would not take me away from the kids.

Hold on a second, though. Why did I even have the mindset and ability to think that way? Was I simply arrogant enough to believe that my connections and relationships would help me avoid prison? I had mentors and friends who were leaders in the community, people who were well known to the judge. Maybe that is why I allowed myself to imagine that house arrest could even be possible.

Why did I have the audacity to believe my sentence might be lighter than someone else's? I had to admit that throughout my life I had watched role models around me ask for more, fight for more, and refuse to settle for less. Perhaps those examples gave me the faith, or maybe the foolishness, to think that I too could ask for more.

But when I listened to David speak with my family and friends, I finally understood the truth. The sentence I received was far less than they had feared I would get. Any other defendant in my situation would likely have faced at least thirty months behind bars.

Yet none of that mattered to me in that moment. All I could think was that I was going to have to leave my kids. The thought hollowed me out from the inside, leaving nothing but fear and heartbreak where hope had once been.

On the ride home, my mom asked me if I was scared. I was scared. But I tried to be resolved. *I am a survivor and a fighter. I can do this.*

What felt like the end of my story was, in truth, the beginning of my transformation. At first, I looked at the evidence as a weapon against me, a tool meant to destroy. Slowly, I began to see it differently. The evidence was a mirror. Every page, every fact, every accusation forced me to confront who I had become and what I had allowed.

In the crushing moments after my sentencing, I could not yet see that a new foundation was being laid. All I could feel was the weight of humiliation, the terror of prison, and the heartbreak of leaving my children. Yet even in that darkness, seeds of meaning were being planted. Seeds I would not recognize until much later. Seeds that would eventually grow into lessons I would carry and share, not just for my own life, but for the lives of countless others.

My grandfather had once been imprisoned with Gandhi. I began to wonder, could my own imprisonment have a purpose too? My uncle's words echoed in me with a clarity I had not felt before: "It's not happening to you. It's happening for you."

The process stripped me bare. It tore away the layers of perfectionism and performance I had worn like armor for decades. It shattered the image I had clung to. I had to fall completely to touch what was real. I had to hit the ground to finally build on something solid. Rock bottom was not the end. It became my foundation.

On the ride home, as we prepared to tell the children about my sentencing, I stared out the window and realized this was not just the end of a chapter. It was the beginning of an entirely new journey, one I could not yet see, one I could not yet imagine, but one I knew would change me forever.

LEADERSHIP LESSONS: WHEN EVERYTHING FALLS APART

1. **Crisis reveals leadership character.** When everything falls apart, what's left isn't your title or achievements but your core values and how you respond. Do you face reality or hide from it? Do you own your mistakes or shift blame? Do you see opportunity in adversity or only loss?
2. **The fall strips away the false.** Crisis removes the facade, revealing what's authentic beneath. Organizations that survive existential threats often discover their true values aren't in mission statements but in how they respond when everything breaks down.
3. **Radical accountability transforms culture.** The willingness to see uncomfortable truths, without defensiveness, is the gateway to reinvention. When leaders model accountability, they create cultures where problems can be addressed before they become catastrophic.
4. **Rock bottom becomes your foundation.** What looks like failure can become the solid ground for something authentic and meaningful. Organizations that survive crisis often emerge stronger precisely because they've been forced to rebuild on truth rather than image.
5. **Purpose emerges from pain.** Our greatest contributions often come from our deepest struggles. Leaders who can transform personal or organizational pain into purpose create a legacy impact that transcends conventional success.

REFLECTION QUESTIONS

- What crisis have you faced that revealed your true leadership character?
- How might your current challenges be happening *for* you rather than *to* you? What purpose might be emerging from your present difficulties?
- If everything external was stripped away—title, status, achievement—what foundation would remain? Is it solid enough to build something meaningful upon?

CHAPTER 4

Seeing with New Eyes

I walked out of the courthouse that June afternoon with the sentence in my chest like a stone. One year and one day in prison. The uncertainty I had lived under was over. What remained was a new, raw work: to make meaning of what lay ahead and to squeeze the life I had into the narrow doorway the calendar had given me.

David told me, "Sixty days." Sixty days to prepare my family, to tie up loose ends, to explain to two small people that their world would look different soon. Sixty days to say things I had left unsaid for years. Sixty days to teach my children how to find me in memory and in the choices I left behind. How do you measure sixty days when time itself feels cruel, reminding you that every sunrise is one step closer to leaving your family behind?

Standing outside the courthouse, my family pressed in around me like a fragile shield, but nothing could soften the blow of what was coming. My chest ached with a grief I could not name, and yet beneath the weight of shame and fear, a small voice whispered that if I could not choose my circumstances, I could still choose how to live them. That night, alone in my kitchen, I stared at the calendar. Sixty days. The numbers blurred through tears until they looked less like dates and more like a ticking bomb. Before sentencing, time had felt endless, uncertain, malleable. Now it was mercilessly defined, a countdown to the day I would lose everything. My parents sat at the table across from me, their faces carved with worry, and I forced the words out, trembling, "I am going to make every day count."

That choice cracked something open in me. The days that followed became unbearably sharp, like glass I had to walk across barefoot. Every hug from my children burned into me, joy and agony tangled together. I began to see what I had been blind to for years. The way Maya's fingers curled around her hair when she was lost in thought. The light in Kyler's eyes when he talked about a book he was reading. The unspoken strength in my parents' silence as they carried me when I could no longer carry myself.

Time no longer expanded. It constricted, pressing in on me, demanding that I finally pay attention. And in that unbearable narrowing, I found something I had never expected. A strange and piercing kind of freedom.

REFRAMING IS A LEADERSHIP SUPERPOWER

That lesson was not just personal. It is the same truth every leader must face. We do not get to choose the crises that arrive at our doorstep. Market downturns, product failures, team conflicts, betrayals, unexpected losses. The list is endless. What separates those who collapse under the weight from those who rise is not the circumstance itself but the perspective they bring to it.

When leaders dare to ask, “What else could this mean?” they do more than manage a crisis. They unlock possibility where others see only ruin. They breathe hope into rooms heavy with fear. They turn endings into beginnings. This kind of reframing does not just spark innovation. It inspires resilience, ignites courage, and opens doors that once looked permanently shut.

But let me be clear. Reframing is not about slapping on a smile or pretending the pain is not real. It is not denial. It is the disciplined, gut-wrenching practice of looking at the same brutal situation from every angle and then making the terrifying choice to lean into the meaning that serves growth instead of destruction.

After my sentencing, I had no choice but to live this truth. The days became a countdown I could not stop. I threw myself into preparing for prison with the same relentless focus I once gave to closing a deal or hitting a target. But this time, achievement was not the goal. My only goal was surrender. To release control, to lay down the armor, to stop fighting what was already decided. And in that surrender, I began to find a different kind of strength.

Those sixty days between sentencing and surrender cracked my life open. They were an unexpected gift wrapped in grief, a forced pause that let me see beyond the frame I had spent years constructing. With the glass shattered and the borders gone, I could finally see what was inside the picture of my life. I began to realize that my desperate grip on perfection had blinded me to the small, sacred moments happening within it. Now, with that frame irreparably broken, I was seeing my life with new eyes.

David had given me a checklist of what to bring, which was almost nothing, what to expect, strip searches, head counts, the loss of privacy, how to handle my affairs before leaving. But no checklist could prepare me for the emotional complexity of getting ready to leave my life.

I can still feel the weight of that afternoon at my dining room table with my baby sister Subha, one week after the sentencing. My house was just across the street from our parents', so we moved between them like we were trying to hold two worlds together.

Subha had flown down from Philadelphia to help me prepare. She is a doctor, married to another doctor, raising two children of her own. She sat across from me while I tried to stitch myself into the future with ink and paper.

Around us, stacks of blank notecards and colorful stickers covered the table like confetti from a celebration we were not having. "One hundred eighty for each of them," I whispered, nodding toward the piles. "One for every school day I might be gone."

Subha nodded, her eyes shining with tears she would not let fall. "That is a lot of notes."

"I know," I said, my voice catching as I picked up a pen. "But they need to feel me even when I am not there."

For days, we worked on those notes. Each one carried a quote I had chosen with care:

"Never, never, never give up." Winston Churchill

"Keep your face to the sunshine and you cannot see a shadow." Helen Keller

"Intelligence plus character, the goal of true education." Dr. Martin

Luther King Jr.

Beneath each quote I wrote a personal message, something meant only for either Kyler or Maya, words that would make them feel seen and known and loved even in my absence. My hands cramped from writing, but I refused to stop. Each note had to be handwritten. They needed something tangible from me, something infused with my presence. I even bought fun stickers to brighten each one.

This was never just about notes for my children. It was about time itself. For the first time in my life, I felt the edges of it pressing in. Sixty days. One hundred eighty school mornings. Every second mattered because it could not be stretched or reclaimed. That clarity was excruciating, but it was also a gift.

URGENCY CLARIFIES PRIORITIES

When time feels finite, focus sharpens. The most effective leaders operate with this sense of urgency not because they are anxious but because they are clear about what matters most. Organizations often drift into complacency when success creates the illusion of infinite time. But markets shift. Technologies disrupt. Opportunities vanish while teams debate minutiae in endless meetings.

Leaders who cultivate a healthy sense of urgency, not panic, but purposeful focus, create cultures that move differently. They make decisions more quickly, execute more effectively, and adapt more nimbly to change.

I carried that same urgency with me into the final days before my surrender. A few nights before I was set to report, I sat with Bekki, my friend since childhood. Friends and family had gathered at my home for what we called a "send-off." The phrase caught in my chest. It felt less like a farewell to freedom and more like I was preparing for a journey I could neither stop nor fully comprehend.

"I'm terrified," I admitted, something I hadn't said aloud to anyone else, not even my parents. "I don't know how I'll survive this." Bekki reached into her pocket and pressed a small black rock into my palm. Engraved on its surface were four simple words: "This too shall pass."

Something shifted in that moment. I made a subtle but profound reframing that would transform my entire prison experience. What if I approached this not as punishment but as purposeful retreat? Not as disconnection but as an opportunity for deeper connection with myself?

I wouldn't be allowed to take the rock with me to prison, but I took a picture of it. That photo, and the perspective it represented, would become an anchor in the months ahead.

THE SHIFT STARTS INSIDE

August 17, 2015. My surrender date. I had three wishes for my last hours of freedom: to run at sunrise with my family, to pray together, and to kiss my children goodbye. We drove to Matheson Hammock Park, where I had run countless Saturday mornings throughout my life. Mom, Dad, and Maya came with me. Kyler was too emotional to leave the house, and I understood. Sometimes the heart knows what it can and cannot bear.

As I jogged the familiar path, watching the sunrise spill gold and pink across the sky, I thought about my name: Rashmi, meaning the rays of the morning sun. Even in this darkest hour, I clung to that meaning, the promise of light, of renewal, of rising again. After my run, we sat together at the water's edge, singing bhajans and praying. The park was still except for our voices and the soft rhythm of waves. In that sacred space, I felt a fragile peace break through the chaos inside me.

My father's voice, steady and strong, carried the prayers he had learned as a boy in India. My mother's hands moved gracefully through the gestures passed down for generations. These rituals were more than tradition. They were anchors, connecting me to resilience far greater than my present circumstances, to the strength that had carried my family through loss, risk, and reinvention.

I thought of my grandfather in his prison cell with Gandhi, how he clung to faith even in confinement. I thought of my parents rebuilding after bankruptcy, holding on to their values when everything else collapsed. This moment by the water was not only about saying goodbye. It was about remembering who I came from and what I carried within me.

Back home, the hardest part awaited. I held Maya and Kyler close for what felt like forever and not nearly long enough. How do you say goodbye to your children when you cannot promise when you will see them again? How do you leave them with strength rather than fear? Maya, only nine, tried to be brave, though I saw the terror in her eyes. She had already endured so much, and now her mother was leaving in a way she could not understand. Kyler, at ten, had read enough John Grisham novels to know something about courts and prisons, but no knowledge could soften the ache of separation. He tried to be strong, to step into the role of protector, even as his own world cracked beneath him.

"I need you both to remember something," I told them, holding their faces in my hands. "I love you more than anything, and I will come back safe to you."

The drive to David's office felt dreamlike. My mother sat beside me, her grief tucked away for my sake. My sister Subha had flown in from Philadelphia to be with me. From the back seat she held my hand in silence, a presence stronger than words.

As we drove through the familiar streets of Miami, I saw my life as if from the outside. The office buildings where I once worked. The restaurants where I had celebrated victories. The neighborhoods where I built my reputation. They looked the same, yet I was not. The woman driving to surrender to federal prison was no longer the attorney who had once moved confidently through these streets.

Months of preparation, of reckoning with shame, of facing fear had brought me here with quiet resolve. This was happening. I could resist it and make it harder, or I could accept it and search for growth within it. At David's office, he reviewed the surrender process one last time: what would happen at the courthouse, what to expect during booking, what the first night might be like. The details made it both painfully real and strangely unreal.

Walking into the federal courthouse, I felt neither brave nor broken. I felt present. Fully present in a way I had not been in years. The perfect child. The successful attorney. The community leader. Those identities had been stripped away. What remained was simpler but stronger: a mother who loved her children, a daughter carrying her family's resilience, a woman stepping into her truth.

PERSPECTIVE IS A CHOICE, NOT A CIRCUMSTANCE

The morning I surrendered to the US Marshals, I stood in handcuffs and shackles, dressed in paper-thin clothing and rubber slip-on shoes. I walked through the underground hallway connecting the Federal Courthouse in Miami to the Federal Detention Center across the street. Each step echoed with finality. I was about to be processed, stripped, and assigned to a housing unit.

The strip search was the moment theory became reality. Standing naked before a female guard, told to bend, squat, and cough, I felt every shred of dignity being peeled away. It was deliberate, methodical, almost ritualistic in its intent to erase the person I had been. In that unbearable moment, my uncle's words from months earlier pierced through the shame. "This is not happening to you. It is happening for you."

For the first time, I understood what he meant. The stripping away of everything external—status, appearance, achievement, control—was forcing me to confront who I really was without the armor I had spent years perfecting. All my identities were being taken: the lawyer, the leader, the success story. What would remain? Who would I be when I could no longer be perfect?

That first night, lying on a thin mattress without a pillow, I could barely see through the narrow slit of a window. But I searched the darkness until I found one faint star. I fixed my gaze on it and held on, remembering the morning's sunrise, the meaning of my name, the reminder that even here, in the starkest of places, light still existed.

I began to sing in my heart, not out loud, but from deep within, the lyrics to "Seasons of Love" from *Rent*:

Five hundred twenty-five thousand six hundred minutes
Five hundred twenty-five thousand moments so dear
Five hundred twenty-five thousand six hundred minutes
How do you measure, measure a year?

One day down. Three hundred and sixty-five to go. But for the first time in my life, I wasn't counting the days to get through them. I was counting them to make them count.

I thought prison would be the end of my story. Instead, it became the beginning of a new one. The good little girl who had tried her whole life to be perfect had finally fallen all the way down. And in that breaking, I began to discover something I had never allowed myself to see. That falling was not final. It was the doorway to rising, to seeing with new eyes, to finding possibility where I had once seen only walls.

Years later, I would stand on stages in front of business leaders and tell them about that moment. I would share how this shift in perspective reshaped not just my prison experience but my entire approach to life and leadership. "Perspective is not something you have," I would say. "It is something you choose. And that choice determines not just how you endure challenge but what you create from it."

The journey from courthouse to prison to purpose was never about circumstances changing. It was about vision shifting. It was about learning to see what had been there all along. The possibility hidden inside pain. The opportunity concealed within limitation. The strength that only emerges when everything else is stripped away.

This is the gift I now carry to leaders who face their own crucibles. To remind them that their stories are not just about surviving, but about transforming. Not just about bouncing back, but about rising into something more authentic, more purposeful, more true than what existed before.

The woman who once measured worth in goals and achievements now leans into authenticity. The lawyer who once built walls of credentials now builds bridges with vulnerability. The mother who once feared absence now knows presence is not proximity but a love that endures through any circumstance.

All of it because of a shift in sight. From punishment to purpose. From ending to beginning. From falling to rising through.

LEADERSHIP LESSONS: SEEING WITH NEW EYES

1. **Reframing is a leadership superpower.** The same situation can be seen as either a crisis or a catalyst. Leaders who can find opportunity in adversity create resilience in their organizations and inspire innovative solutions.
2. **Urgency clarifies priorities.** When time is limited, focus sharpens. The most effective leaders operate with a healthy sense of urgency not because they're anxious, but because they're clear about what matters most.
3. **The shift starts inside.** Culture change, innovation, and organizational transformation begin with internal shifts in how people see themselves, their work, and each other, not with external strategies or restructuring plans.
4. **Perspective is a choice, not a circumstance.** How leaders frame challenges determines not just how

their teams experience them but what they create from them. This mindset shift transforms victim thinking into agency and innovation.

REFLECTION QUESTIONS

- What situation in your life or business are you currently viewing as a limitation that might actually be an opportunity? How might reframing this challenge reveal new possibilities?
- When was the last time you operated with true urgency, and how did it clarify your priorities? What distractions might you eliminate if you approached your current goals with that same focus?
- What mindset shifts have transformed your own leadership journey? How have you helped others make similar perspective shifts?

PRISON PIZZA

INGREDIENTS

- 1 pack flour tortillas
- 1 packet Sazón seasoning
- Salsa
- Ketchup
- Onion powder
- Garlic powder
- Italian seasoning
- Sausage (optional)
- Tomato (optional)
- Onion (optional)
- Bell pepper (optional)
- Pepperoni (if available)
- 1 block mozzarella cheese (for shredding)

PROCESS

1. Slightly dampen the flour tortillas with water.
2. Place them in a clean garbage bag, add Sazón, and shake until evenly coated.
3. In a bowl, mix salsa and ketchup with onion powder, garlic powder, and Italian seasoning to create the sauce.
4. Spread the sauce mixture evenly over each tortilla.
5. Add toppings: sausage, tomato, onion, bell pepper, and pepperoni.
6. Shred mozzarella from the block and sprinkle generously on top.
7. Place the pizzas on a piece of clean cardboard.
8. Microwave on high for 10–15 minutes, until cheese is melted and bubbly.
9. Let cool briefly, then enjoy your homemade Prison Pizza.

PART 2

Identify

In the midst of challenge, we discover that rising is never a solo act. It is shaped by the people who surround us, the ones who hold us steady when the ground beneath us feels unsteady. The Identify pillar of the RISE Framework is about recognizing those people, the ones who ground us in our values, lift us when we falter, and hold up mirrors that reveal both our brilliance and our blind spots. When everything else feels uncertain, authentic connection becomes the strongest anchor.

Identifying our tribes and truth-tellers is not just personal; it is strategic. We become like the voices we allow closest to us. Choosing who speaks into our lives directly shapes our capacity for growth and resilience. These relationships give us the psychological safety to risk vulnerability and the honest feedback required for true transformation.

When my world collapsed, I discovered who really saw me. Not the lawyer. Not the mother. Not the mistake. Just me. Their presence became the foundation for my rebuilding. What I learned is that community does more than comfort us through hard times. It shapes who we become because of them. By intentionally identifying the people who call us higher, even when it stings, we create the kind of connection that turns isolation into belonging and performance into purpose.

CHAPTER 5

Rooted in Belonging

My earliest memories are bathed in warmth and belonging. I grew up held by the arms of a community that felt like an extension of family. Weekends meant gathering with other Indian families, the air thick with the scent of cardamom and cumin, laughter spilling from every corner, and bhajans softly weaving through the hum of conversation. The "aunties" and "uncles" who surrounded me were not bound by blood but by something deeper, shared history, shared hope, and a kind of love that asked for nothing in return. Their hugs lingered, their voices carried comfort, and in their presence, I felt completely seen and safe.

TRUE BELONGING ISN'T PERFORMANCE-BASED, IT'S PRESENCE-BASED

In those weekend gatherings, we prayed together in pujas, sang bhajans until the walls seemed to hum with devotion, shared steaming plates of homemade food, and created a sense of belonging that felt effortless and whole. I grew up surrounded by people who celebrated me with unfiltered pride. Every debate tournament, every academic award, every new leadership role became a collective victory. Their joy felt genuine, their pride sincere, and I basked in it.

But somewhere along the way, I began to believe that love had to be earned. When an auntie would beam with pride while telling others about my latest success, or when an uncle would introduce me at temple as "the one who's going to be a lawyer," a quiet belief took root inside me. I began to confuse their pride with my worth. I thought I was loved because of what I achieved, not simply because of who I was.

I remember sitting cross-legged on the cool marble floor of the temple, watching my father work alongside other members of our community to establish the first Hindu Temple of South Florida. For him, it was never just about building a place of worship. It was about building a foundation, a home where children growing up between worlds could belong without question. What I didn't yet understand was that this belonging had never been conditional. It didn't require perfection to preserve it. It didn't disappear when the achievements stopped.

The same truth holds in organizations. When leaders tie recognition and value solely to performance metrics and achievements, people start to believe their worth is conditional. Belonging begins to crumble under the weight of expectation. True connection, whether in a family or a company, can only thrive where people feel valued not for their output, but for their humanity.

True belonging at work begins when people feel seen and valued for their full humanity, their creativity, their perspective, their flaws, and their character, not just for what they produce.

UNCONDITIONAL SUPPORT ACCELERATES GROWTH

When my father arrived in America in 1967, he could have easily been dismissed as just another struggling immigrant. Instead, he met Ms. English Helen Bagby, the grand dame of Chapel Hill, who saw his potential and chose to invest in his success without any guarantee of return.

Helen Bagby became more than a landlady. She became family, so much so that she later became my godmother. When I was born, my parents chose Helen as my middle name in her honor. She helped us find our place in a foreign world, not because of what we might achieve but because she recognized our inherent worth and dignity.

Helen's guidance was invaluable precisely because it came without conditions. My father could ask her about American customs, social norms, and professional expectations without fear of being judged as inadequate. She created a kind of psychological safety that allowed him to learn, make mistakes, and grow authentically.

Years later, I would recognize this as one of my earliest lessons in what true support looks like. Helen's care was unconditional, her investment born not of expectation but of belief. It was love that asked for nothing in return, rooted in the simple act of seeing potential in another human being.

That kind of mentorship changes people. It reshapes how they see themselves and what they believe they are capable of becoming. In organizational settings, the same truth applies. When leaders create environments where people feel safe to learn, fail, and grow without fear of judgment, they unlock something deeper than performance. They create cultures where authenticity, innovation, and trust can thrive.

That lesson was not only about mentorship. It echoed in my own home. Our family was not just a unit; we were a team built on mutual support and shared purpose. I watched my parents study law together, raise children, build businesses, and teach us as they went. But even in this loving environment, quiet self-imposed messages about worthiness began to take shape. They would stay with me for decades and influence how I understood belonging.

The family business became a classroom for relationship building but also for understanding value through productivity. Whether it was helping at my parents' flea market stall or sitting at the dining table as they discussed their latest real estate venture, I learned about connection and contribution. But I also internalized the belief that my value came from what I contributed, how well I helped, how much I learned, and how quickly I could adapt to what was needed.

I spent weekends helping in my parents' office, at flea markets, and around other Indian families. That hustle and camaraderie shaped me, but I began to believe that the praise and affection I received were directly tied to how helpful I was, how well I performed my assigned tasks, and how little trouble I caused.

Every weekend, my sister and I helped my mother sell imported clothing and accessories. I watched her interact with customers with genuine warmth and care, building relationships that transcended transactions. But when customers complimented me, saying, "What a smart, helpful daughter you have," I absorbed the message that being smart and helpful was what made me lovable.

What I didn't understand then was that being seen meant being recognized for my full self, not just my achievements. This misunderstanding about the source of love and belonging creates similar dynamics in organizational settings. When recognition and value are tied primarily to performance metrics, people begin to believe their worth is conditional. They start performing instead of contributing authentically, leading to burnout, reduced creativity, and diminished results.

AUTHENTIC FEEDBACK CREATES AUTHENTIC LEADERS

Throughout my childhood, my father served as my most consistent mirror, though it took me years to understand what he was actually reflecting back to me. I remember sitting at the kitchen table, struggling with advanced math problems, ready to give up. My father sat beside me, not solving the problems but asking questions that helped me find my own way through.

At the time, I thought he was praising my intelligence, reinforcing the idea that I was valuable because I was smart. What I understand now is that he was reflecting back my inherent capability, not tied to any particular achievement, but as a fundamental truth about who I was. His confidence wasn't in my performance; it was in my essence.

My parents' voices became my inner compass: "Beta, you can do anything" from my father, balanced with "Do it right as best as you can" from my mother, ambition tempered with integrity. But I heard these as performance expectations rather than expressions of unconditional faith in my character and potential.

When Kyler and Maya were born, they became the most honest mirrors in my life. Children don't see titles or achievements; they see presence or absence, attention or distraction, authenticity or performance. Their eyes reflected the truth of who I was being, not what I was accomplishing. They loved me not for what I achieved but for how I showed up, or didn't.

The most effective leaders create these same kinds of authentic feedback systems in their organizations. They build cultures where people feel safe to reflect reality, both positive and challenging, back to leadership.

These mirror moments are not only about performance metrics. They are about the full impact of leadership presence, character, and authentic engagement. They invite us to look beyond what we accomplish and examine who we are while accomplishing it. True leadership reflection requires us to confront difficult questions. How do we show up when things fall apart? Do we lead from ego or from empathy? Do we create belonging, or do we demand perfection?

Years later, when the FBI walked into my office and the world I had built began to crumble, those questions came rushing back. Everything I had depended on to define myself, my profession, my reputation, my image of success, fell away in an instant. In that unraveling, I faced the truest test of belonging. Was I loved only for the roles I played, or for the person I was beneath them?

As the titles and status disappeared, I discovered something both painful and beautiful. The people who had truly seen me all along, beyond the résumé and the perfection, stepped forward. They held space for me in my breaking. They reminded me that belonging rooted in authenticity cannot be taken away. It endures, even when everything else falls apart.

VULNERABILITY DEEPENS CONNECTION

When I finally made the decision to plead guilty, I had to make the hardest phone calls of my life. One by one, I called friends, family members, and colleagues to tell them about my case. With every ring, my chest tightened. I braced myself for judgment, disappointment, and the quiet withdrawal of love. I was no longer the successful attorney, the community leader, the perfect daughter they had once celebrated. I was the woman who had fallen.

But what I expected to be a series of losses became something very different. Person after person met my confession not with condemnation but with compassion. Some paused in silence before sharing their own stories of failure and regret. Others cried with me, offering words that felt like lifelines. Many told me that my honesty had given them permission to be honest about their own struggles. By losing my perfect image, I had unknowingly created the space for connection that my perfectionism had always kept at a distance.

That season of calls broke something open in me. For the first time, I realized that love and acceptance were not things I had to earn. In that raw and humbling moment, stripped of titles and status, I found not rejection but a deeper acceptance than I had ever known. The community I feared would turn away instead surrounded me with more love than I had ever experienced during the height of my success. They showed me that their pride had never been about my achievements. I had simply misunderstood the source of their affection.

Months later, standing in the prison yard at Coleman Correctional Complex, I would return to that lesson again and again. Everything external had been taken from me. My law degree, my reputation, my curated image of success. But something remained untouched, something no sentence could take away. It was my capacity for connection, for belonging, for love that did not depend on achievement or perfection.

The communities that shaped me, my family, our Indian circle, my chosen friends, had never loved me because I was perfect. They had loved me through my imperfections, through my pride, through my fall. Even when I could not see it, they had always valued who I was beneath the striving.

Now, when I work with organizations facing change, conflict, or crisis, I bring that truth with me. Sustainable cultures are not built on shared performance metrics or common success stories. They are built on trust, psychological safety, and the kind of authenticity that makes people feel seen beyond their output. True belonging in an organization does not come from flawless execution. It comes from shared humanity.

The most resilient teams are the ones where people feel valued for their full selves, their creativity, their perspective, their flaws, their character, and their potential, not just their productivity. When belonging is conditional on performance, people waste their energy managing their image instead of contributing their gifts.

The perfect child who once believed she had to earn love through achievement now knows that her real power lies in helping others recognize their unconditional worth. The professional who once sought validation through performance now helps leaders build cultures where authenticity fuels innovation. The mother who once feared that failure would make her unlovable now shows her children that we belong not because we are perfect, but because we are imperfect and loved anyway.

Most of all, I now understand what my grandfather knew in that prison cell with Gandhi. We carry our community within us not because of what we accomplish, but because of who we are. Belonging is not about fitting into someone else's frame. It is about being fully seen and unconditionally loved for exactly who we are.

LEADERSHIP LESSONS: ROOTED IN BELONGING

1. **True belonging isn't performance-based, it's presence-based.** Organizations that tie recognition and value primarily to performance metrics create cultures where people perform rather than contribute authentically. Sustainable cultures are built on psychological safety and the recognition that every person brings inherent value that transcends their current productivity.
2. **Unconditional support accelerates growth.** Leaders who create environments where people feel safe to learn, make mistakes, and grow without fear of judgment build foundations for genuine innovation and sustained engagement. When belonging feels

conditional, energy goes toward managing image rather than contributing authentic gifts.

3. **Authentic feedback creates authentic leaders.** The most effective leaders build cultures where people feel safe to reflect reality, both positive and challenging, back to leadership. These "mirror moments" focus not just on performance metrics but on the full impact of leadership presence, character, and authentic engagement.
4. **Vulnerability deepens connection.** When you stop performing perfection and share your authentic struggles, you can discover a deeper acceptance than you've ever known. Leaders who model appropriate vulnerability create space for others to bring their full humanity to work, leading to stronger teams and more innovative solutions.

REFLECTION QUESTIONS

- Where in your leadership or organization might people feel their worth is conditional on performance? How could you create more environments where people feel valued for their full humanity, their creativity, perspectives, and character, not just their current output?
- Think of a time when someone offered you unconditional support during a difficult period. What specific actions made you feel truly seen and valued? How

might you extend that same quality of support to others in your professional relationships?

- When have you discovered that your assumptions about others' expectations were wrong? How might you be projecting conditional acceptance onto relationships or situations where the acceptance is actually unconditional? What would change if you operated from that different understanding?

CHAPTER 6

The People Who See You Through

We all need guiding lights, the people whose steady love and quiet strength help us find our way when we lose sight of ourselves. In the darkest moments, when fear blurs direction and shame clouds the horizon, it is their presence that becomes our compass.

The people around us either pull us closer to who we are meant to be or keep us anchored to who we once were. But the rare ones, the ones who truly change us, do something deeper. They love us with such consistency that we begin to believe in our own worth again. Their faith in us becomes the mirror that reflects the courage, clarity, and compassion we had forgotten we carried.

These are the people who remind us how to lead with heart. They teach us that love is not a soft skill but a source of strength, that patience is not weakness but wisdom, and that clarity is not found in certainty but in presence.

YOUR CONSTELLATION OF STARS HELPS DEFINE WHO YOU ARE

My parents have always been my North Star, constant and unwavering, the quiet force that has guided me home no matter how lost I became. Even when I could not see them through the storms of my own making, their love never wavered. It remained steady, a light that refused to dim.

When our family faced bankruptcy during my senior year of high school, I watched both of them navigate crisis with calm and grace. There was no panic, no blame, no hiding. They did not shield me and my sisters from the truth, but they also did not weigh us down with fear. Instead, they modeled what it means to face reality with honesty and hope.

"This is temporary," my mother would say as she packed boxes, moving us from our waterfront home into a small rental with the same care she brought to everything. "We will rebuild. We will come back from this." Her words were not empty promises. They were conviction wrapped in love.

My father's faith never faltered, even when I saw quiet sadness in his eyes. He carried his grief privately so he could show up for us with steadiness and strength. He never pretended that what was happening was easy, but he made sure we never doubted that we would find our way through it together.

That balance of truth and hope became the foundation for how I would one day learn to lead through my own crises. They showed me that leadership is not about control or denial, but about the courage to face pain while holding on to purpose. It is the art of acknowledging difficulty while still choosing faith.

Both of my parents taught me that leadership is not about having all the answers. It is about standing steady in the unknown and refusing to let fear dictate your next step. When their business collapsed, they did not know if they would ever recover financially. When I was indicted, they did not know if their daughter would go to prison. Yet in both moments, they responded with the same quiet strength, the same unshakable love that did not depend on the outcome.

The most profound lesson came when I had to call and tell them about the FBI investigation. My hands trembled as I dialed, my voice cracking as I spoke the words I never thought I would have to say. I expected disappointment, anger, even shame. Instead, my father's first words were, "We will get through this together." Not "How could you?" Not "What will people think?" Just that calm, steady promise. His love was not fragile. His faith in me did not vanish with my mistake.

My mother's response was equally powerful. Within hours she was researching criminal defense attorneys, reading articles, and learning the process. Not because she believed I was guilty, but because she wanted to understand the system well enough to protect me. While I sat paralyzed by fear, she moved forward with quiet determination. She did not deny what was happening. She met it with action, clarity, and grace.

Their responses became my model for leadership in moments of crisis. **Lead with love first.** Respond with patience and clear thinking. Hold steady so others can find their footing.

The constellation of people who guided me extended beyond my parents but followed the same pattern. Each one embodied faithful presence. Their love was not conditional on my performance or dependent on my success. It came from a deeper place, the kind of love that holds you when the rest of the world walks away.

During the darkest chapter of my legal battle, these guiding lights did not just offer support. They modeled how to keep hope alive when life feels unrecognizable, how to think clearly when emotions threaten to take over, and how to act with integrity when the stakes are at their highest. They did not help me survive my fall. They taught me how to rebuild from it. They showed me the power of faith over fear, patience over panic, clarity over confusion, and love that transcends every circumstance.

Today, when I work with leaders facing their own moments of collapse, I help them find their constellation. Who are the people who tell them the truth when it is hard to hear? Who models the qualities they most want to embody under pressure? Who believes in their potential even when they cannot see it themselves?

Because in the end, every one of us needs guiding lights. Not only in times of crisis but in the ordinary days between them. We need people whose steady presence reminds us who we are and helps us navigate toward our best selves, especially when the temptation to give up feels strongest.

CULTURE IS FELT, NOT DECLARED

Not all mirrors reflect truth. In the law firms and investment banks where I began my career, I studied senior women closely, watching how they contorted themselves to survive in male-dominated spaces. Their voices carried a practiced rhythm, firm enough to be heard but never so strong as to be labeled difficult. Their suits were elegant but never too striking, their confidence measured, their presence controlled. It was a delicate choreography of belonging without threatening, achieving without overshadowing, existing without taking up too much space.

I learned the steps quickly. I believed that this was the price of admission into the world I wanted to enter. To belong, I had to bend. To succeed, I had to silence parts of myself. This pattern seeped into my cultural identity too. Raised in a vibrant Indian household filled with tradition, music, and meaning, I began to keep that world separate from my professional one.

Even as a child, I had felt the pull to belong elsewhere. I gravitated toward my Western friends because it felt easier, safer. My insecurities told me that being too Indian, too different, would make me stand out for the wrong reasons. I ran from what made me unique, convinced that assimilation equaled acceptance. That need to blend in followed me to the University of North Carolina, to Morgan Stanley, and later to Columbia Law School. Looking back now, I can see that imposter syndrome was driving the entire journey. I never truly believed I belonged, and the more I tried to prove that I did, the emptier I felt.

It is painful to admit how deeply I internalized this belief. Even though my values, goals, and outlook on life were all shaped by my cultural roots, I convinced myself that surrounding myself with other Indian friends would somehow make me appear smaller. I thought it would make me seem less interesting, less modern, less powerful. I was wrong.

The pressure extended far beyond social identity. As the eldest daughter, I felt the weight of every choice. My success would either open doors for my sisters or quietly close them. If I soared, it was proof that women could excel. If I stumbled, it would reinforce every old narrative we were fighting to break.

And then, my children arrived. Kyler and Maya changed everything. They became my why, the heartbeat behind every ambition, the grounding force through every storm. When they were born, success took on a new meaning. It was no longer about proving my worth. It was about protecting theirs. Yet, in my frantic pursuit of stability and security, I lost the very thing they needed most. I missed their moments. I missed their now.

My Miami social circle only deepened this illusion. On the surface, it was a portrait of success, filled with glamorous events and polished appearances. Behind the smiles was exhaustion, debt, and the quiet fear that if we stopped performing, it would all disappear. We went to dinners we could not afford, ordered wine we did not need, and smiled through the guilt of pretending everything was fine. I am ashamed to admit how much I let perception dictate my priorities. I was chasing validation disguised as belonging.

It took losing it all to understand that true belonging does not require performance. It requires presence. The friendships that remained after my fall were not the ones made in luxury dining rooms or networking events. They were the ones forged in vulnerability, the ones built on truth rather than image.

Great leaders know that real connection is not born from pressure or competition but from belief and trust. Teams do not thrive because they are pushed harder. They thrive because they feel seen, valued, and safe. Belonging fuels performance in ways that incentives never can. I witnessed this in reverse. A community built on appearance cannot hold under the weight of crisis. Only authenticity can.

Organizations often make the same mistake that I once did. They assume culture lives in mission statements, value posters, or company handbooks. But culture is not what hangs on a wall. It is what happens in moments of crisis. It is whether people feel safe enough to struggle, to fail, to be human.

True belonging happens when people do not have to leave any part of themselves behind to fit in. It is not the diversity policy that creates culture but the daily practice of empathy and truth-telling. The moments when someone feels free to be fully themselves and knows they will still belong.

The most effective cultures are those where people can bring their full humanity, including their struggles, their cultural identities, and their authentic perspectives, without fear of judgment or exclusion.

TRUST IS BUILT IN SMALL, CONSISTENT MOMENTS

Trust isn't built in grand gestures. It's built in small, consistent moments of showing up for people, reliably and without condition. That is where lasting influence begins. Though all around us we are experiencing the reality that some human technical skills can be replicated and automated, what remains irreplaceable is human connection. The ability to build trust. The awareness to read nuance. The courage to respond with empathy when circumstances are complex.

When Kendall Coffey recommended that David Markus take over my criminal defense, I felt an immediate sense of certainty. I had known David for more than twenty years, since our time teaching together at the University of Miami School of Law. We were not close friends, but there was mutual respect and quiet trust, which soon became essential.

Late one Saturday night, after a dinner meeting with Kendall, I finally made the call. It was close to ten o'clock, and fear pressed down on me like a weight I could not lift. David called back within minutes. He was at a party, yet his tone was calm and focused. We arranged to meet Monday morning.

That Monday, David was direct but kind. He acknowledged that representing someone he had known personally would be emotionally complex, but he promised to bring his full focus to my defense. His honesty built trust instantly. I knew he would not protect my feelings at the expense of my future.

"I need you to understand," he said quietly, "that this will be hard for me too. We have known each other for a long time. But my job is to stay objective so I can defend you well." I nodded, knowing I was in the right hands.

What surprised me was that compassion also came from the other side of the courtroom.

Joe Capone, the prosecutor assigned to my case, could have seen me only as a name on a file. Yet from our first meeting, he showed me something different. After I decided to plead guilty in August 2014, David arranged for us to meet a few weeks later. I walked into that conference room terrified. This man held my future in his hands. But Joe was calm, measured, and fair. He asked difficult questions but listened to every answer. He treated me as a person who had made painful mistakes, not as a problem to be solved.

During one of our breaks, David leaned over and said, "You are doing well. He can see you are being honest."

Over the next several months, Joe and I built an unlikely respect. We spent hundreds of hours preparing for my testimony as the government's main witness at my co-defendant's trial. Though we stood on opposite sides of the legal system, we connected through a shared commitment to do the right thing.

On the day of my sentencing, I saw that connection take on a life of its own. Just before court began, Joe entered the defense preparation room. I expected tension. Instead, he walked toward me and embraced me. It was unexpected and genuine, the kind of gesture that said more than words ever could. I will never forget that moment.

It taught me something essential about humanity. Even within systems built for opposition, compassion can exist. Accountability does not require cruelty. Integrity does not mean detachment. Empathy is not weakness; it is strength. Artificial intelligence can process data and mimic communication, but it cannot replicate the grace of human understanding. True connection remains our greatest advantage.

The people who stood beside me when my life unraveled showed me what belonging really means. Their presence was not transactional. They were not there because it benefited them. They showed up because they cared. That kind of connection cannot be designed by policy or sustained by performance. It grows in spaces where people feel genuinely valued for who they are, not just for what they do.

Organizations that nurture this level of connection thrive because people bring their full creativity and conviction to their work. When people feel seen and trusted, they no longer operate from fear. They create, collaborate, and innovate from a place of safety and meaning.

On the morning of my surrender, August 17, 2015, David confirmed that he had checked twice with the Bureau of Prisons that I was designated to the Federal Detention Center in Miami. Both times, they assured him it was correct.

That morning, as my mother, my sister, David, and I sat for hours outside the U.S. Marshals' office, I saw him step away to speak to a Marshal. His expression changed. When he returned, his eyes told me before his words did.

"There has been a mistake," he said softly. "You were designated to Coleman, not Miami."

Because of that error, I would have to surrender in Miami and wait to be transported to Coleman. What should have been a five-hour drive with family turned into an indefinite wait inside the system.

David immediately filed an emergency motion requesting that I be allowed to drive to Coleman myself. Joe supported it. The judge denied it almost immediately.

The next day, after my first night in prison, Margot came to see me. Her face was pale, her smile forced. She handed me a Diet Coke and a Snickers bar, small comforts in a place that had none.

Then she told me the motion had been denied. I felt the air leave my body. But she stayed. She did not try to fix it or fill the silence. She simply stayed.

That moment revealed a painful truth. The system was built for efficiency, not for humanity. Bureaucracy was the language, not compassion. And yet, even inside that machinery, people like David, Joe, and Margot brought humanity back to it. They fought for me not because they had to, but because they cared.

That is the essence of real connection. It cannot be replicated or replaced.

HUMAN CONNECTION IS YOUR COMPETITIVE EDGE

Community is not proven in success. It is revealed in struggle. The people who surrounded me when everything fell apart taught me that worth is not tied to outcome, and love is not contingent on performance. It shows itself most clearly when everything else has been stripped away.

That truth changed the way I lead and the way I live. In both business and life, we are taught to hide our struggles to preserve credibility. But what if strength is found not in the appearance of perfection, but in the willingness to be real?

Leaders who are honest about their challenges, who admit when they do not have the answer, who ask for help when it matters most, build cultures that thrive. In that honesty, trust takes root. And in that trust, people find the freedom to innovate, to create, and to grow.

The people who stayed with me did not do so because I was untouchable. They stayed because I was human. In their eyes, I found something stronger than success: connection grounded in truth.

The mirrors that mattered most were not the ones reflecting my perfect image. They were the ones that revealed my real self. In my father's steady faith, my children's pure love, and my friends' quiet presence, I saw the person I was always meant to be.

"You cannot grow what you cannot see," I tell leaders now. "Surround yourself with people who tell you the truth, especially when it is hard to hear. The ones who challenge you to rise higher, even when it stings, are the ones who will help you become who you are meant to be."

LEADERSHIP LESSONS: THE PEOPLE WHO SEE YOU THROUGH

1. **Your constellation of stars helps define who you are.** The caliber of people around you will either stretch you into your potential or shrink you into your patterns. Audit your inner circle. Do they challenge you to grow or reinforce your limitations?
2. **Culture is felt, not declared.** People don't stay for perks; they stay where they feel seen and valued. A sense of belonging drives engagement more than any mission statement or corporate benefit. Create environments where people feel genuinely connected to purpose and to each other.
3. **Trust is built in small, consistent moments.** Whether in business or in life, showing up for people, reliably and without condition, is what creates lasting influence. Grand gestures don't compare to consistent presence.
4. **Human connection is your competitive edge.** In an era of AI and automation, genuine relationships and empathy will set your business apart. Invest in developing your team's emotional intelligence and relationship skills as strategically as you invest in technical capabilities.

REFLECTION QUESTIONS

- Who in your life serves as a mirror, reflecting back to you who you truly are? How do you respond to this reflection, especially when it's uncomfortable?
- Think about a time when someone showed up for you during a difficult period. What specific actions made you feel supported? How might you translate those behaviors into your leadership?
- When was the last time you modeled appropriate vulnerability as a leader? What impact did this have on your team?

CHAPTER 7

Anchors in the Darkest Places

IDENTIFY ANCHORS OF AUTHENTIC VOICES

Finding anchors in unfamiliar waters is not just about survival. It is about remembering who you are when everything familiar falls away. In prison, this truth became my daily reality, but it is equally vital in every environment where change feels relentless. The most resilient organizations understand this instinctively. When people are forced to navigate disruption, they need connection points that remind them of stability, meaning, and belonging.

For some, anchors take the form of routine, a morning ritual, a shared meal, a walk at sunset. For others, they live in relationships that remind them they are seen and valued beyond their output. The most effective leaders know how to preserve these anchors during times of transformation. They understand that stability in one area gives people the courage to adapt in another.

Prison stripped away every layer of identity I had built. My title, my clothes, my control, my carefully curated image, all gone. There was no stage left to perform on, no armor to protect me. I became inmate 05121-104, a number stitched above my heart. Standing in that fluorescent light with the smell of bleach hanging in the air, I was forced to confront myself without any of the roles or labels I had clung to. Who was I when there was nothing left to prove?

The loudest sound in prison was not the slam of metal doors or the echo of footsteps down concrete corridors. It was silence. The kind of silence that comes from women who have learned that speaking carries consequences. I noticed it almost immediately after arriving at the Federal Detention Center in Miami. Women moved through the unit quietly, their eyes lowered, their shoulders slightly hunched. When a guard entered the room, conversations stopped mid-sentence. The stillness that followed was heavy and sharp, a silence made of fear.

That silence taught me more about leadership than any corporate boardroom ever had. Silence does not mean agreement. It often means people are afraid. I have seen the same pattern in law firms, boardrooms, and executive teams where people stay quiet to protect themselves. Organizations mistake compliance for commitment, but fear always kills truth before it can take root. Great leaders listen for what is not being said. They know that when people feel safe enough to speak freely, innovation and trust begin to grow.

My night at the detention center were a blur of exhaustion and confusion. My room was in the farthest corner of the unit. The metal bed was bare, and the air smelled of chemicals and sweat. There was no pillow, so I searched empty rooms until I found a thin, stained mattress pad that smelled of mildew. It was a small victory, but it gave me something to hold on to, a shred of comfort in an unfamiliar world.

On my second day, I met Lucie, a former mayor convicted on similar charges. When I was reassigned to a different room, she was already there, making her bed with careful precision.

"You must be Rashmi," she said, her tone gentle but strong. "I have been expecting you."

Lucie became my first friend and guide. She lent me small things I did not yet have—soap, toothpaste, a comb. She explained the rhythms of prison life, the unwritten rules that kept you safe, and the subtle hierarchies that governed the unit. Most of all, she shared her faith. Every morning she prayed on her knees, whispering words of gratitude and hope. "This is just a season," she would tell me. "Not your life."

Lucie had lost everything she once thought defined her: her position, her reputation, her freedom. Yet she carried herself with quiet strength, offering kindness instead of bitterness. She had become a mother figure to many of the women inside, guiding them not with authority but with love. Watching her helped me see that leadership is not a title or a role. It is how you show up when everything else has been stripped away.

After ten days, Lucie and I were both told to pack up. We were being transported. They woke us at midnight to begin the process. I was handcuffed, shackled, and fitted with a waist chain that locked my wrists to my sides. Along with about fifteen other women, I was loaded onto a bus bound for Coleman.

The ride was long and dehumanizing. The air was thick, the seats were metal, and movement was nearly impossible. At one point, an older woman named Margaret tried to use the bathroom. Still in chains, she could not manage, and her urine spread across the floor. For three hours I held my feet up to keep them dry, staring out the small window, thinking about how fragile dignity really is.

When we arrived at Coleman, the process began again. Intake, processing, paperwork, waiting. By the time I reached my housing unit, I was drained. I was assigned to cube 405 and met my new bunkmate, Michelle. She smiled and offered me coffee. "I make it my own special way," she said. "Chocolate, coffee, and just the right amount of sugar."

That first cup of Michelle's coffee tasted like warmth itself. Each afternoon, we sat together during count, sipping from our cups and talking about our children, our pasts, our hopes. That simple ritual became my anchor.

Then came Patricia, whom everyone called Mom. A former office manager at a law firm, she carried herself with quiet authority and maternal grace. She became my mentor and protector, a steady presence who reminded me daily that I was still a mother, still a daughter, still human. When I wept after a painful phone call with my children, she held me and whispered, "You are still their mother, Rashmi. Nothing changes that."

Patricia taught me how to crochet when I wanted to make Christmas gifts for my children. "It is not about the blanket," she said, placing the yarn in my hands. "It is about who you become while you make it." Each stitch became a meditation, a rhythm that slowed my thoughts and softened my fear. As my hands moved, something in me began to heal.

The crochet table became a circle of connection. Women from every background sat together, weaving their own stories into the patterns. We did not share a common past, but we shared a longing for meaning and love. In that circle, I learned that community is built not through grand speeches or policies but through shared creation.

Patricia's leadership was unlike any I had ever experienced. She guided without control. She corrected without judgment. She cared for the women around her as whole human beings, not as problems to manage. She embodied a truth I now teach leaders everywhere. Real leadership is not about what gets done. It is about who people become in the process.

When she saw me struggle with a mistake, she smiled and said, "You cannot move forward until you fix what went wrong." In that moment, I realized she was talking about far more than crochet.

Those women, those moments, and those small acts of grace became my anchors. They reminded me that even in the most dehumanizing environments, we can still find humanity. We can still build belonging. We can still rise through it, one connection at a time.

Finding your voice requires losing the mask. The most effective leaders lead with both strength and softness, owning their truth without needing to prove it.

When we create environments where people must minimize parts of themselves to belong, we do more than harm individuals. We weaken the whole. Every time someone hides a piece of who they are, we lose a perspective that could bring new ideas, deeper understanding, and genuine innovation. The strength of any community, whether inside an organization or behind prison walls, depends on the truth it allows to exist.

Teaching became one of my unexpected anchors at Coleman. After volunteering to help women prepare for their GED exams, I was offered a formal position as a math teacher. The classroom was small and spare, with plastic chairs, old tables, and worn textbooks. Yet within those four walls, something extraordinary happened.

Women who had spent their lives believing they were not smart enough began to discover what had always been there. I watched them light up when a problem finally made sense, their pride flooding the room. I remember one grandmother who cried when she understood fractions for the first time. "Nadie nunca me explicó así," she whispered. "No one ever explained it to me like this." In that moment, I realized that teaching was not about instruction. It was about reflection. It was about helping someone see themselves clearly, often for the first time.

Teaching also gave me back my voice. In a place that rewarded silence, the classroom required me to speak with strength and care. I had to guide, to correct, to encourage, and to believe. The act of teaching became an act of remembering who I was.

One day, Valerie came running into my cube, her eyes wide with joy. "I passed," she said. "I passed the math section." She wanted to give me something from commissary to thank me. I smiled and told her, "You already did." Her success was my reward.

The truth was that I had privileges others did not. My family supported me. My commissary account was full. Many women had no one left on the outside. That difference sat heavily with me. It reminded me that leadership is never about how much we have, but about how much we give.

Real empowerment is not something one person grants to another. It happens when people begin to see their own power. My best moments as a teacher were not when I explained something perfectly, but when a woman looked at me and said, "I get it now."

CREATE SPACE FOR AUTHENTIC COMMUNITY

That truth extended beyond the classroom. One evening, news spread that Tiffany, a woman in her forties, had been diagnosed with advanced breast cancer after years of being ignored by the prison's medical staff. When she returned from her first chemotherapy treatment, she was shaking and pale. Without a word, the women around her moved into action.

Someone brought blankets. Another smuggled crackers from the kitchen. A third, who had survived her own cancer, stayed by her side through the night. Another person took her laundry and washed it by hand. We created a circle of care, quiet and unspoken.

No one assigned these roles. There was no authority, no direction, no expectation of reward. There was only compassion.

That moment changed how I understood community. True resilience is not built by policy or position. It is built by people who care. The most effective organizations recognize and protect this kind of organic connection. They understand that during crisis, humanity will always outperform hierarchy.

Some of the most powerful leadership I witnessed in prison came from women who never sought recognition. There was Luz, the seamstress who measured every new arrival for uniforms and whispered encouragement while she worked. There was an elderly woman who kept an informal library in her locker, tracking borrowed books in a small notebook so that everyone could read. These women led not through control, but through constancy. Their quiet presence gave order and comfort to those around them.

They taught me that influence does not depend on titles or charisma. It grows through steady acts of service and reliability. Great organizations often overlook this kind of leadership, mistaking visibility for value. Yet the people who sustain culture are often the ones who simply show up, again and again, doing small things that make others feel seen.

About a month into my sentence, I began writing a daily email called "Quote of the Day" to my approved contact list on the outside. Each morning, I found a passage that spoke to me and wrote a few reflections. It became my morning ritual, a way to make meaning of my confinement and stay connected with the world beyond the gates.

One morning, I shared a quote from Viktor Frankl: "Everything can be taken from a person but one thing, the freedom to choose one's attitude in any given circumstance." I wrote about finding purpose, even in confinement, and about the small moments of grace that appeared when I looked for them.

The responses I received filled me with gratitude. Friends told me that my words helped them through their own struggles. In that exchange, I found a renewed sense of purpose. My voice still mattered. Even here, I could contribute.

These moments taught me something about empowerment that applies everywhere. Permission does not come from the outside. It comes from within. I could not wait for approval or ideal conditions. I had to choose to speak and to use what I had where I was.

Organizations that cultivate this kind of permission unlock a deeper kind of engagement. When people feel trusted to speak honestly, to contribute without fear, and to express their truth, they stop performing and start creating. They begin to see themselves as partners rather than employees.

What I learned at Coleman continues to shape how I teach and lead today. Whether in a prison or a boardroom, people crave the same things, to be seen, to be valued, and to know that what they bring matters. When leaders create spaces where those needs are met, transformation begins to take root.

RECOGNIZE WISDOM IN UNEXPECTED SOURCES

During my time at Coleman, my attorney told me there was another case in Tampa where I might be called to testify. He explained that if I agreed, there was a chance I could come home early and avoid the halfway house and house arrest. It felt like a small window of hope, so I said yes.

When I told the women at Coleman about it, several warned me about what it meant to be sent to county jail. "That place is rough," one said. "They send people there as punishment. You do not want to go." I listened as they described filthy cells, endless noise, and guards who looked the other way. Some of them had been sent there after fights or for having contraband, and the fear in their eyes told me everything.

In my mind, county jail became the bottom of the system, the place where people were sent when they no longer belonged anywhere else. I told myself I did not belong there. I was different. I had made mistakes, but I still believed that my background and education set me apart.

On the morning of my transfer, I was handcuffed, shackled, and fitted with a waist chain that connected my wrists to my sides. The metal bit into my skin as I walked in line with the others toward the waiting transport van. Pride and fear battled inside me. I still held on to the idea that I was not like the women around me.

The ride to Pasco County Jail was long and quiet. When we finally arrived, the sound hit me first. Doors slamming, voices shouting, the constant buzz of fluorescent lights. The smell of bleach mixed with sweat and something sour. I felt disoriented, stripped of the fragile sense of control I had managed to hold at Coleman.

One evening, after dinner, a group of us gathered to watch the movie *Burlesque* with Christina Aguilera and Cher. For two hours, we lost ourselves in the music, the glitter, and the story of resilience. When the credits began to roll, the room was filled with an energy that felt rare.

Then one woman turned to me and said, "Hey, you must know how to Bollywood dance, right?"

I laughed. "Of course. That is practically required at every Indian wedding. I might not be trained, but I can definitely dance Bollywood."

"Then teach us," she said. She started humming a popular Bollywood song in mainstream music.

So I did.

We pushed aside the plastic chairs and cleared a little space on the cold concrete floor. The harsh fluorescent lights became our stage lights. I showed them how to move their hands and hips, how to let the rhythm take over. We laughed until we could hardly breathe. For a few minutes, we were not inmates. We were women dancing, free and unguarded, finding joy where it should not have existed.

When the music faded, I looked around at the faces of the women beside me. There was a woman who had survived years of addiction and prostitution. There was another who had spent much of her life homeless. There was a young mother of twenty-four, serving time for selling meth while her little boy waited for her at home.

In my old life, I would have judged them. I would have seen them as people who had made bad choices, people whose stories had nothing to do with mine. But standing there with them, I felt the truth rise inside me. How *dare* I pass judgment on these women? Who was I to think I was better? But for the grace of God, there go I.

The illusion of difference dissolved. We were all the same. We were women who had made mistakes, who carried guilt and grief, who wanted redemption and peace. The line between us had never been real. It was only pride that had built it.

For twenty-three days in county jail, I cooked, prayed, cried, laughed, and danced with those women. We became a small family, bound together by shared vulnerability and the simple act of caring for one another. Each day softened me a little more, stripping away judgment and replacing it with compassion.

Every night, as the lights dimmed and the noise faded, I lay on my bunk and thought about what I had learned. Judgment and compassion cannot live in the same heart. One closes it, the other opens it. These women had shown me what grace looks like in action. They had given me a glimpse of my own humanity reflected back through theirs.

I had arrived at county convinced I did not belong there. I left knowing that belonging is not about where you are. It is about seeing yourself in others and allowing yourself to be seen in return.

This realization has profound implications for leadership. **When we recognize that we are all fundamentally connected, that the boundaries we create between departments, hierarchical levels, or professional identities are ultimately artificial, we lead differently.** We become more compassionate, more inclusive, more willing to listen and learn from those we might otherwise dismiss.

As I reflect on what sustained me through those months of confinement, first at the Federal Detention Center in Miami, then at Coleman, and briefly at Pasco County Jail, the answer is clear: relationships. Not the superficial connections we often form in professional settings but deep bonds of mutual care and authentic seeing.

Lucie, who shared her belongings and wisdom those first difficult days in Miami. Patricia, who mothered me when I needed it most and taught me to create with my hands. Kamala, who helped me reconnect with my cultural roots and spiritual practices. The women I taught, who reminded me of the power of witnessing potential. The collective response to Tiffany's cancer diagnosis, which demonstrated our shared humanity. The quieter presences who created beauty, maintained resources, and offered consistent kindness.

These relationships weren't built on achievement or status. They didn't depend on what I could produce or provide. They formed through authentic presence, through a willingness to be seen in both strength and vulnerability, through genuine care that transcended differences in background and circumstance.

The prison system itself is designed to isolate and dehumanize. Yet within that system, women created webs of connection that maintained our humanity and dignity. If this is possible in the most constrained and controlling environment, imagine what becomes possible when we intentionally foster authentic connection in our workplaces, communities, and families.

When everything else was stripped away—status, possessions, freedom—what remained were these anchoring relationships. They taught me that we are never as alone as we feel in our darkest moments, that connection can form in the most unlikely places, and that our capacity to rise depends not just on individual resilience but on the strength of the hands holding us up.

LEADERSHIP LESSONS: ANCHORS IN THE DARKEST PLACES

1. **Identify anchors of authentic voices.** During organizational transformation, people need psychological stability points to navigate uncertainty. Effective leaders intentionally preserve certain routines, relationships, or spaces that remain constant while everything else changes. These strategic anchors aren't about resisting change; they're about creating the security that enables people to adapt more effectively.
2. **Create space for authentic community.** True cohesion rarely develops through team-building exercises or value statements alone. The deepest organizational bonds form when people engage in meaningful shared activities, solving real problems, creating solutions, or building something of value together.
3. **Recognize wisdom in unexpected sources.** Organizations that limit their definition of "expertise" to credentials, positions, or specific backgrounds miss critical insights. The most innovative companies actively seek wisdom from unexpected sources, frontline workers, new hires, people from different industries, or those with nontraditional backgrounds.

REFLECTION QUESTIONS

- Where in your organization do you see support networks operating outside formal structures? How might you recognize and strengthen these organic connections?
- What shared activities in your organization naturally build community? How might you create more opportunities for people to make, solve, or create together?
- What perspective-giving touchpoints might help your team maintain clarity during challenging times? How can you help people find these points of orientation when everything else seems uncertain?

PRISON TAMALES

INGREDIENTS

- 1 bag Fritos corn chips
- 1 bag spicy hot Cheetos (or substitute Doritos or any spicy chips)
- Hot water (enough to moisten)
- Hot sauce (to taste)

PROCESS

1. Crush the Fritos and Cheetos inside their bags until finely crumbled.
2. Combine both bags of chips into one larger bag.
3. Slowly pour in enough hot water to create a thick, dough-like mush.
4. Knead the mixture inside the bag until evenly blended.
5. Drain any excess water carefully.
6. Press and roll the mixture inside the bag into the shape of a traditional tamale.
7. Let the bag sit for about 5 minutes to firm up.
8. Remove the rolled tamale from the bag and drizzle with hot sauce.
9. Slice and enjoy your Prison Tamale.

PART 3

Surrender

Surrender is the most counterintuitive step in the RISE Framework. It goes against everything we are taught about control, achievement, and success. We grow up believing that strength means fighting harder, pushing even more, and never letting go. Yet true surrender asks something far more courageous. It asks us to release what no longer serves us, the need for control, the trap of ego, the illusion of perfection, and the fear of being seen as vulnerable.

Surrender is not weakness. It is not giving up. It is the strength to loosen our grip on the images and expectations that confine us. When we release the need to appear flawless, we begin to experience life, as it truly is. Only in that release can we discover a deeper kind of freedom.

This pillar challenges us to recognize the difference between what we can change and what we must accept. It invites us to set down ego, certainty, and judgment. It reminds us that growth sometimes comes not from striving for more but from letting go of what no longer belongs. Surrender is the quiet act of removing what blocks our truth so that our true power can rise.

The most effective leaders understand this. Real influence often comes not from control but from clarity and trust. Leaders who can release the need to dominate outcomes create space for creativity, empathy, and collaboration to flourish.

In prison, everything external was taken from me. My title, my possessions, my public identity, all stripped away. What remained was only me, raw and unguarded. And in that stillness, something began to shift. Surrender created space for authenticity to emerge. When I stopped performing, I could finally be present. When I acknowledged my vulnerability, it became a bridge to connection instead of a source of shame. When I began to tell myself the truth, it became the foundation for transformation.

Surrender is not where the story ends. It is where the real story begins.

CHAPTER 8

Quiet Acts of Surrender

The battered suitcase sat open on the bed in my mother's childhood home in Rewari, India. At just eighteen years old, she carefully folded a few saris, tucked in photographs of her family, and slipped a handful of books between the layers of fabric. Each item was a piece of the world she was about to leave behind.

A month earlier, she had met my father for the first time. It had been an arranged meeting, one she had tried to resist, but now she was surrendering to a new reality. The decision was not hers alone, yet she carried it with quiet strength.

She left behind her dreams of attending the London School of Economics, her close-knit family, and the familiar rhythms of her life in India. As she boarded the plane to America, her heart held both hope and heartbreak. The air smelled of jet fuel and possibility. The hum of the engines carried her toward a life she could not yet imagine.

In those early months in her new country, oceans and the cost of long-distance calls kept her separated from her family. She filled notebooks with letters home, her handwriting looping across thin blue aerograms. Her words were filled with optimism, describing the excitement of discovery and the beauty of this strange new land. But beneath the ink and polite descriptions lived something she rarely shared: the ache of loneliness, the quiet courage of starting over, and the silent surrender of a young woman remaking herself far from everything she knew.

TRUE LEADERSHIP STARTS WITH RADICAL HONESTY

For me, surrender meant releasing the frame itself, letting go of how my life was supposed to look, and embracing what it actually was. My mother had understood this long before I did, when she left India and surrendered the image of the life she thought she would have. Now I stood at my own crossroads, facing a future I could not control. I had lost all the titles I had worked so hard to earn. Could I loosen my grip on the perfect image I had spent years curating? Could I find freedom not by fixing my circumstances but by accepting them and choosing authenticity instead?

Organizations facing disruptive change often make the same mistake my mother avoided. They attempt partial transformations, adjusting structures while clinging to outdated mindsets, adopting new technologies while preserving harmful cultures, and announcing bold visions while quietly resisting what true change demands. Real transformation begins with a full and honest reckoning. It requires the courage to name reality completely, even when that reality threatens our identity or comfort.

My mother never pretended that leaving India was not a loss. She grieved privately, allowing herself to feel the pain of what she was giving up, while still moving forward with conviction. Her honesty about what she was losing allowed her to embrace what was coming. It was this quiet integrity that kept her from living divided between what was and what could be.

The same principle applies to leadership. The executives I work with often struggle with this first act of surrender: the willingness to name their organization's full reality without defensiveness or denial. They show me glossy strategic plans that mask dysfunction. They talk about market competition while ignoring toxic workplace behaviors. They speak about innovation while refusing to acknowledge their own resistance to change. True leadership begins with radical honesty. It means seeing things exactly as they are, not as we wish they were. This level of truth-telling requires humility, but it also unlocks freedom.

Honesty is not only about identifying problems. It also means recognizing unexpected strengths, unspoken opportunities, and paradoxes that do not fit our preferred narratives. The leaders who learn to surrender to reality, in its entirety, lay the foundation for authentic transformation. They stop trying to control perception and begin engaging with truth.

My father's journey to America began with his own act of surrender. In 1967, he arrived carrying a small bag of dirt from his village in Beri, a symbol of the roots he refused to forget. Before leaving India, he made three promises to his mother, my dadiji. He would not eat meat, he would not drink alcohol, and he would not be intimate with women. These vows were his way of anchoring himself in identity while stepping into uncertainty.

What inspires me most about my father's story is not only his determination to succeed but his willingness to surrender what he thought he knew. Before coming to America, he was a respected student at one of India's most prestigious technical institutes. Once here, he had to learn everything anew, how to speak, how to eat, how to belong. Living in a rented room above the home of Ms. Helen Bagby, a Southern woman who would later become my godmother, he allowed himself to become a student of culture and humility.

He asked questions most people would be too proud to ask.

"Where should I take a girl on a date?"

"Is macaroni and cheese supposed to be eaten with ketchup?"

"How do I respond when someone says 'How are you' but keeps walking?"

Each question represented a surrender of ego, an admission of not knowing. That humility became his greatest strength. By surrendering the need to appear competent, he created space to grow competent.

Leaders face the same challenge today. Those who have built their careers on certainty and expertise must now lead in times that demand adaptability and learning. The ones who thrive are those who surrender the safety of always being right and embrace the vulnerability of continuous discovery.

This kind of surrender does not diminish authority; it redefines it. When leaders can say, "I do not know yet, but I am willing to learn," they create environments where others feel safe to do the same. They replace performance with curiosity, hierarchy with collaboration, and fear with trust.

I have seen this distinction vividly in organizations navigating rapid technological change. Leaders who cling to old models make decisions rooted in pride rather than awareness. They dismiss insights from younger voices or unconventional thinkers. But those who surrender the illusion of being the smartest person in the room unlock collective intelligence and creativity. They stop managing from control and start leading from connection.

My father approached America as an engineer approaches a problem, breaking it down piece by piece until he understood it. What others saw as impossible barriers, he saw as data points to be studied. His methodical mindset gave him the clarity to adapt without losing himself.

Three years later, he returned to India determined to marry and bring a partner into this new life. My mother arrived in 1970 with quiet courage, carrying her own form of rebellion and grace. While my father had years to adjust to the American way of life, she had to absorb it all at once: new country, new marriage, graduate school, and soon motherhood. I was born twelve months after she arrived, and my sister came thirteen months later.

Together, my parents built a life that balanced adaptation with authenticity. They held on to their roots while learning to grow in foreign soil. From them, I learned that surrender does not mean erasing who you are. It means allowing yourself to evolve while carrying forward what matters most.

LETTING GO OF EGO CREATES ROOM FOR EVOLUTION

The most profound act of surrender in my family's history came in the mid-1980s when my parents lost everything in the market crash. We moved from our 8,400-square-foot Italian marble waterfront home to a 1,000-square-foot rental near my high school. The financial devastation was complete. Their real estate portfolio had vanished, and they made the painful decision to file for bankruptcy.

I was a senior in high school when my parents sat me down to explain what had happened. It was a crushing blow not only to our finances but to their identity and pride. Within our Indian community, where success was often equated with respect, bankruptcy felt like public humiliation.

Yet even in crisis, my parents held tightly to their values. Some friends disappeared, unable or unwilling to face our new reality. But the ones who stayed surrounded us with love, showing us what real friendship looks like when everything else falls apart.

One day, I woke early and walked quietly down the narrow hallway of our small rental house. As I passed the bathroom, I heard a sound that stopped me cold. My father was crying. His muffled sobs echoed through the door. I froze, listening to the man who had always seemed unshakable weep alone in the bathtub.

Years later, he told me he would go into the bathroom to cry because it was the only place he could be alone, away from my mother and us three girls. He felt like he had failed. I have thought often about what creates that belief, that deep internal conviction that failure makes us unworthy of love or respect.

When my own world collapsed, I finally understood my father's tears. When everything I had built fell apart—my law career, my reputation, my freedom—I felt the same weight of failure. I found myself crying in hidden corners, overwhelmed by the distance between who I thought I was and the truth I could no longer deny.

In those moments, I understood the loneliness of shame, the way it isolates and silences you. I realized how easily we mistake a single chapter for the whole story. The difference between my father and me was circumstance. His collapse came from forces outside his control: the market, the economy, the unpredictable swings of real estate.

Mine came from choices I made, ethical boundaries I ignored, and moments I justified. Yet the shame felt identical. We both had to face the humbling truth that strength is not the absence of failure but the willingness to face it with honesty.

This kind of pain is not confined to Indian families or immigrant expectations. Across every culture, losing money or declaring bankruptcy carries a stigma that cuts deep. My parents felt as though they had let down not only themselves but everyone who believed in them.

What still moves me most about that time is the quiet resilience they displayed. The same man who wept in the bathtub emerged each morning composed, ready to face the world again. My mother, calm and steady, held our family together, finding dignity in the smallest acts of care and consistency. Their private pain did not diminish their public strength. It gave it depth.

From them, I learned that authentic leadership is not about never breaking. It is about breaking and choosing to rise again with humility, grace, and truth.

True strength includes moments of acknowledged weakness,

and resilience isn't about never breaking but about how we put ourselves back together.

DENIAL ISN'T STRATEGY, IT'S SABOTAGE

The surrender to accountability, choosing the harder path of integrity over the easier path of legal absolution, embodies a leadership principle that many organizations struggle to embrace. Denial is not strategy. It is sabotage. When leaders avoid uncomfortable truths, they trade temporary comfort for lasting harm.

I have worked with many organizations where leaders refused to confront unethical behavior, toxic personalities, or strategic mistakes until the cost became impossible to ignore. The pattern is always the same. Small denials grow into large disconnections from reality until the distance becomes too wide to bridge without deep and painful change.

My parents modeled something different. They faced their financial collapse directly, without minimizing its impact or shifting blame. Their honest reckoning became the foundation for authentic rebuilding. They did not avoid difficult conversations with investors or creditors. They did not pretend the situation was better than it was. They surrendered the comfort of denial for the clarity and transformation that only truth can bring.

In the aftermath of bankruptcy, I watched them rebuild with new purpose. My father began practicing law, my mother started new ventures, and together they worked with a deeper understanding of both success and failure. Their reputation for integrity became their most valuable asset. When they started over, doors opened because people remembered how they had handled adversity.

Through every challenge, my parents held on to their faith. Each morning began with prayer. Each decision was made with reflection. Each setback was seen as part of a greater purpose beyond immediate understanding. Their faith never wavered, even when everything else did. They surrendered outcomes to God and taught us to trust that light would return, even in darkness. Their surrender was not passive acceptance. It was active faith, a decision to find peace in purpose rather than control.

Years later, when my own world collapsed under the weight of the FBI investigation, indictment, and imprisonment, my parents' example became my anchor. I watched them navigate the shame and stigma of having a daughter convicted of a federal crime with the same grace and quiet strength they had shown during their own hardship.

The night before my sentencing, my mother and father performed a small puja, a Hindu prayer ritual, at their altar. Their movements were calm and deliberate as we lit the oil lamp and placed flowers and incense. We did not need to speak about what the next day would bring. I knew what they were teaching me. It was the same surrender they had modeled my entire life, not surrender to defeat, but to a greater wisdom and trust.

"Whatever happens tomorrow," they said softly, "we face it together."

That night, I felt their faith surround me like light. It was not ceremony for the sake of appearance. It was real. When I stood in the courtroom the next morning and heard the judge sentence me to prison, I could still feel the strength of that faith in my chest. It steadied me. It reminded me that surrender was not the same as loss. It was the beginning of transformation.

This same truth applies to leadership. The most powerful leaders are not those with perfect résumés or polished appearances. They are the ones who own their full story, including the mistakes and struggles that shaped them. Their authenticity draws others in because people can sense the alignment between their words and their truth.

Since my release from prison, I have learned that owning my story, especially the parts I once wanted to hide, creates connection in ways perfection never could. People do not respond to performance. They respond to truth. They recognize their own humanity in the honesty of another person who has fallen, faced it, and chosen to rise.

This principle transforms organizations when leaders live it fully. Teams respond differently to executives who admit when they are learning, who share their own failures as openly as their successes, who create space for others to bring their whole selves to work instead of a curated version of perfection. When authenticity becomes the standard, culture shifts from performance to purpose.

AUTHENTICITY IS MAGNETIC

One of the most profound surrenders of my life came in August 2014 when I sat in David Markus's office with my parents as he and his partner, Margot, laid out the harsh reality of my federal case. Hour by hour, as they methodically dismantled each potential defense, I felt the story I had been clinging to begin to dissolve. The belief that I was innocent, misunderstood, or unfairly targeted could no longer stand against the weight of the evidence.

It was the hardest surrender of my life. For the first time, I had to admit not only to others but to myself that I had crossed ethical lines.

I had to accept that I was accountable for my choices and that I was not a victim of circumstance. In that moment, I surrendered the need to be right and chose instead to face the truth. Letting go of control over the story I had created became the foundation for everything that came after.

Surrendering to the truth was terrifying. I had built my identity on being the perfect child, the straight A student, the community leader. How could I now accept that I was a criminal? But as the days passed after that meeting, I began to feel something unexpected. Beneath the fear was a strange sense of freedom, the kind that only comes when you stop fighting reality and finally face it.

My decision to plead guilty was not only a legal one. It was a moral reckoning. I stopped resisting the truth and started embracing it fully, without denial, without excuses, and without the exhausting weight of justification.

That surrender created room for something new to take root. I began connecting with people from a place of honesty instead of performance. I reached out to friends, family, and colleagues to tell them about my case before they could learn about it elsewhere. I expected rejection. Instead, I found compassion. Person after person responded not with judgment but with understanding. Many shared their own stories of struggle, regret, and redemption. By releasing the image of perfection, I opened the door to authentic connection that my carefully managed facade had never allowed.

This experience revealed something that would later shape my work with leaders. When people release the exhausting need to appear flawless, they create cultures where truth can exist. They turn failure into a source of learning rather than a reason for shame. I have seen this pattern repeatedly in organizations. Leaders who pretend to have all the answers create fear. Leaders who can admit when they do not know or when they have failed create trust, innovation, and resilience.

Telling my children about my guilty plea required another form of surrender. I had to let go of their image of me as the perfect mother. I wanted to shield them from pain, but I realized that what they needed most was truth. By being honest, I gave them something more meaningful than protection. I gave them permission to see that love is not rooted in perfection. It is rooted in truth.

The sixty days between my plea and my surrender date became a time of quiet transformation. I had already given up my law license, my professional identity, and my community status. I let go of control over my children's lives and the illusion that I could shape how others saw me. Each release brought new clarity. I began to see myself not as a collection of achievements or mistakes but as a human being in progress, flawed yet worthy, broken yet whole.

On the morning of my surrender, August 17, 2015, I surrendered not only to the reality of imprisonment but also to the belief that this painful experience might someday hold purpose. My uncle's words from months earlier echoed in my mind. "Beti, one day you will understand that this is not happening to you. It is happening for you."

That shift in perspective became the ultimate surrender, not only accepting reality but trusting that even pain could serve as a teacher. It is a lesson I now share with leaders who are navigating disruption or uncertainty. Every challenge can be seen not as a punishment but as an invitation to grow.

When I walked into the federal courthouse later that morning, I felt a calmness that surprised me. The months of reflection, acceptance, and truth-telling had carried me to a place of quiet strength. I understood that this was happening and that my choice was simple. I could fight it and make it harder, or I could accept it and rise through it.

The surrender process was both exactly what I expected and something far beyond words. The physical details were routine: the handcuffs, the shackles, the stripping away of freedom. Yet the emotional experience was deeper than I could have imagined.

Sometimes we have to lose everything we think we are in order to discover who we truly are. Sometimes the bottom of our life becomes the foundation for our becoming.

LEADERSHIP LESSONS: QUIET ACTS OF SURRENDER

1. **True leadership starts with radical honesty.** Authentic transformation begins with radical honesty. Organizations that filter reality through defensive lenses or avoid confronting uncomfortable truths limit their capacity for meaningful change. The most effective leaders create cultures where naming reality, without blame or defensiveness, is valued as the essential first step toward transformation.
2. **Letting go of ego creates room for evolution.** The ego's need to be right, to know, to maintain status blocks the adaptive learning essential for growth. Leaders who model the courage to say, "I don't know," to seek input from unexpected sources, and to acknowledge their

learning edges create organizations capable of continuous reinvention.

3. **Denial isn't strategy, it's sabotage.** When leaders avoid uncomfortable truths, they trade short-term comfort for long-term damage. Organizations that encourage honest reckoning with setbacks, ethical lapses, or strategic missteps develop greater resilience than those that maintain comforting fictions. The energy required to maintain denial drains resources that could be directed toward meaningful solutions.
4. **Authenticity is magnetic.** Leaders who own their full stories, including mistakes, struggles, and lessons learned through failure, create connections that polished performances cannot. Their authenticity attracts others who sense the alignment between words and lived experience. Organizations led by authentic leaders enjoy deeper trust, greater engagement, and more meaningful collaboration.

REFLECTION QUESTIONS

- What uncomfortable truths might you be avoiding in your organization or team? What would change if you surrendered the comfort of denial for the clarity of honest assessment?
- Think of a time when you witnessed authentic leadership during a crisis. How did that leader's willingness to surrender control, certainty, or ego influence the team's response and resilience?
- What parts of your own leadership story have you been reluctant to share? How might selective vulnerability, sharing appropriate struggles and lessons learned, strengthen rather than diminish your influence?

CHAPTER 9

Shedding the Armor

In the stillness of my prison cell, with every external identifier stripped away, I was left with nothing familiar. No designer clothes. No prestigious title. No carefully crafted image. For the first time in my life, I faced the question that had always been buried beneath the noise of achievement. Who am I without the armor?

The process was terrifying. Each layer of protection had been built slowly over years of striving. Every mask I wore had served a purpose. Each piece of armor had shielded a part of me I was too afraid to reveal. My ambition protected my fear of failure. My perfectionism disguised my longing to be accepted. My success hid the quiet voice that wondered if I was ever enough.

To remove that armor felt like standing exposed before the truth. Every defense I had relied on—the credentials, the accomplishments, the need to prove myself—began to fall away. What remained was something raw and unfamiliar but undeniably real.

In that silence, I realized that everything I had believed made me strong had also kept me distant. The very things I had built to protect myself had imprisoned me in an image I no longer recognized.

And now, with nothing left to hide behind, I was finally free to meet myself.

RECOGNIZE OUR IMPERFECTIONS

The morning light filters through the blinds of my childhood bedroom in Miami. I am standing in front of the mirror, a nervous seventh grader trying on clothes for the first day of school. Three outfits are scattered across my bed. Not too nerdy. Not too trendy. Not too much attention, but not invisible either.

"Rashmi, you will be late," my mother calls out.

I grab a Carnation Breakfast Bar from my desk drawer, knowing I will not have time for a proper breakfast. I glance at the clock. Twenty minutes before we need to leave, and I still have not decided which version of myself I will present to the world today.

Even at that age, I was already perfecting the art of adjustment. I knew how to fit in, how to smile, how to say the right thing. I could sense what people wanted from me and become it. But standing there in front of the mirror, I remember feeling the quiet exhaustion of not knowing who I really was beneath the layers.

I lived in a cultural split that defined my early years. Indian at home, American outside. Moving between these worlds became second nature, smooth on the surface but filled with friction underneath. At home, I was the obedient Indian daughter who spoke Hindi when asked, helped with pujas, and followed traditions without question. At school, I became the assertive American student who led clubs, debated fiercely, and earned straight As.

The weight of this dual identity was invisible to everyone but me. Every day felt like an unspoken performance, a constant calculation about which parts of myself were acceptable and which needed to stay hidden. I learned to read the room before I learned to read for pleasure.

What I did not see then was how this pattern was quietly shaping my perfectionism. Every outfit, every grade, every word became part of a lifelong attempt to be flawless. I equated being accepted with being without fault. But beneath the surface of all that striving lived a deep fear that my true self might not be enough.

It took me years to understand that perfection is not connection. The cracks, the doubts, the moments of insecurity are what make us real. Standing in that mirror, I thought I was preparing for school, but what I was really learning was how to perform.

That pattern of perfection followed me into adulthood. It showed up in my work, in my relationships, and in my leadership. I tried to be the woman who always had it together, who never faltered, who could carry everyone's expectations with a steady smile. But pretending to be perfect only distanced me from myself and from others.

What I know now is that imperfection is not failure. It is the doorway to authenticity. When we stop striving to appear flawless, we create space for truth. When we stop pretending to be who we think others want us to be, we finally begin to meet who we really are.

OWNING OUR TRUE SELVES

Recognizing our imperfections is where authenticity begins. When we divide ourselves into carefully managed versions, we create the conditions for insecurity and mistrust. The energy spent maintaining those divisions drains what could instead be used for connection, creativity, and growth.

My relationship with my body became one of the earliest battlegrounds in my search for acceptance. I have struggled with body image for as long as I can remember, always feeling too big, too brown, too different from the blond, slender version of beauty that filled magazines and television screens in the 1980s and 1990s.

Middle school was especially cruel. I was overweight, and my last name seemed impossible for teachers to pronounce correctly. The combination of my appearance and my otherness made me an easy target.

"King Tutt, Bahama Butt," a boy once shouted as I walked down the hallway. The laughter that followed still echoes somewhere inside me. It was another reason to build a perfect exterior, another layer of armor to protect a tender heart.

By high school, I decided to try out for the cheerleading squad. Not because I loved cheerleading but because I thought it might finally make me belong. I remember standing in line at tryouts, watching girls execute effortless jumps and high kicks that my body could not quite match. But I was determined. I practiced relentlessly, pushing myself to prove that I deserved to be there. I could not do the splits or the flips, but I could be loud. I could smile. I could perform every move with focus and precision.

Somehow, I made the team. But even that small victory brought new anxiety. "For the game on Friday, we are all wearing the white skirts," the cheer captain announced. My stomach dropped. The uniforms exposed my legs, and I saw only flaws when I looked in the mirror. The cellulite, the shape, the imperfections. I felt different all over again.

So I found a solution. Pantyhose. I wore them under my uniform, believing they would hide what I did not want others to see. Of course, pantyhose were not part of the uniform. They made me stand out, not blend in. But in my mind, the embarrassment of breaking the rules was easier than the vulnerability of revealing my imperfect body.

That physical armor was simply another version of my emotional one. The pantyhose were not about modesty. They were about fear. Fear of rejection. Fear of being seen as less than. Fear that if people noticed my flaws, they would confirm what I already believed about myself, that I was not enough.

I see that same fear reflected in leaders who armor themselves in different ways. They hide behind titles, expertise, or a polished image of certainty. They speak in rehearsed language, avoiding emotion. They believe that any glimpse of imperfection will cost them respect. But the truth is the opposite. People do not follow perfection. They follow what is real.

When leaders allow themselves to be fully human, they create permission for others to do the same. When they acknowledge mistakes, share what they have learned, or show vulnerability, they build trust. That trust fuels innovation and courage because people no longer fear being wrong. They see that their leader is not performing strength but living it.

For me, perhaps the most painful armor I built was around my cultural identity. I used to be embarrassed that I was Indian.

There, I have said it.

Even now, those words still bring a flush of shame to my face. But they are true. Back then, being Indian was not something to celebrate. Most of my classmates could not tell the difference between India and Pakistan, Hindu and Muslim. To them, everything foreign blended into one stereotype, something to laugh at or misunderstand.

"Does your family own a 7-Eleven?" one classmate asked.

"No," I said, forcing a smile.

"Oh, then a motel?" she replied, laughing as if she had made a clever joke.

When Indira Gandhi was assassinated, a boy in my class asked if she was my aunt. The ignorance was endless, and I did not yet have the confidence to correct it. Instead, I absorbed it, allowing it to shape how I saw myself.

I tried to erase the difference. I spent hours begging my mother to buy me the clothes everyone else wore. Guess jeans, Keds, leg warmers, anything that would help me blend in. I straightened or permed my hair, adjusted my clothes and attitude, and did everything I could to seem less foreign. I thought belonging meant assimilation.

In college, that belief only deepened. Despite the presence of a vibrant Indian Student Association, I kept my distance. I wanted to fit in, and fitting in meant being as American as possible. I told myself it was ambition, but in truth, it was shame. I believed that success in America required shedding anything that marked me as different. I thought that to truly belong I needed to erase parts of myself.

Owning my true self has taken decades. It has meant peeling away layers of fear, shame, and conditioning. It has meant standing in rooms where I once tried to blend in and choosing to take up space instead.

It has meant seeing my body, my culture, and my voice as sources of strength rather than flaws to conceal.

Authenticity is not found in perfection. It is found in wholeness. It begins the moment we stop editing ourselves to meet expectations and start showing up as the full expression of who we are. That is where connection, creativity, and real leadership begin. I see similar patterns in organizations where employees from underrepresented groups feel pressured to "code-switch" or downplay their cultural backgrounds to advance. The resulting psychological toll doesn't just hurt individuals; it robs organizations of the innovation and perspective that diversity promises.

My journey back to embracing my cultural identity didn't happen overnight. It was a gradual process of recognizing that what I once perceived as limitation was actually strength, that my dual heritage gave me perspectives and capabilities others lacked.

SHAME THRIVES IN SILENCE

The most innovative organizations are those where people feel safe to experiment, to fail, and to learn in public. That kind of safety begins with honesty, both collective and personal.

Even as a teenager, I struggled with this. During our difficult financial years in high school, I was consumed by the fear of what people might think. I remember my prom night vividly. My date was coming to pick me up at our small rental home, far from the grand waterfront house where we used to live. I wasn't ashamed of my family, never that, but I was terrified that he would see me differently once he saw where we lived.

Would he notice the worn furniture? Would he compare this modest living room to the marble floors we once had? Would he silently judge me?

As his car pulled into the driveway, my heart pounded. The anxiety wasn't about the house itself. It was about the image I had built around myself. I had worked so hard to project confidence, success, and stability. And now, all of it felt like it was about to collapse under the weight of reality.

He never said a word about the house. He probably didn't even notice the things I obsessed over. But the shame I carried in that moment revealed something important about how much energy I had invested in appearances. What I didn't understand then was that silence feeds shame. I never told anyone about how hard it was for my family. I never spoke about the stress or fear. I never gave myself permission to be vulnerable. And in that silence, the shame grew stronger.

Years later, when I was running my own law practice, that same pattern reappeared. On the surface, everything looked perfect. I was building a successful business, raising two beautiful children, and contributing to my community. But behind the scenes, I was exhausted and anxious. The financial pressure was immense, and I refused to ask for help. I could not let anyone see that the successful attorney everyone admired was struggling to keep it all together.

I see now that silence, my own expectations, assumptions I made, and limiting beliefs were my prison. I wore perfection like armor, believing it protected me, but it was slowly suffocating me. I measured my worth through external signs: the neighborhood we lived in, the car I drove, the schools my children attended. None of it reflected who I truly was or what mattered most.

I am ashamed that I allowed society's definition of success to drown out my own. The house, the car, the appearances, none of it could fill the growing emptiness inside. But what I regret even more is the silence. The unwillingness to tell the truth. The failure to ask for support. The belief that struggles made me unworthy of love or respect.

That silence didn't just live in me; it mirrored what I later observed in organizations everywhere. Leaders who feel they must appear infallible create cultures where no one feels safe to tell the truth. When image becomes more important than integrity, problems fester until they erupt. Innovation dies because risk feels dangerous. People burn out trying to meet impossible standards that no one can sustain.

True leadership begins when we replace performance with presence. When we admit what is hard. When we invite others to share what is real. It is not weakness to speak the truth about our challenges; it is the first act of courage.

Shame thrives in silence. When we voice reality, we create opportunities for collaborative solutions and authentic transformation.

Perhaps the deepest source of my shame came from the gradual betrayal of my own core values. I had always prided myself on integrity, honesty, and doing the right thing. My grandfather had been imprisoned alongside Gandhi while fighting for India's independence, and moral courage was woven into my family's story.

AUTHENTIC LEADERSHIP BEGINS WHEN WE STOP PERFORMING AND START LIVING OUR VALUES

Yet in my quest for success and validation, I made compromises that gradually eroded these values. When red flags arose with this client,

I looked the other way. When ethical questions surfaced, I found justifications. I told myself that everyone was making these same compromises, that this was simply how business worked in the real world.

This rationalization was a form of armor, too, protecting me from confronting the growing gap between who I claimed to be and how I was actually living. Each small compromise made the next one easier, until I found myself making decisions I would have once condemned. Authentic leadership begins when we stop performing and start living our values.

The shame I felt wasn't just about legal consequences or public embarrassment. It was about recognizing how far I had strayed from my own moral compass. The most painful moment wasn't standing before the judge; it was standing before myself and acknowledging that I had known better.

This moral drift happens in organizations too. Companies with strong mission statements and values slowly allow expedience to erode principle. What begins as an exception becomes common practice. The rationalization that "everyone does it" replaces the harder question: Is this who we said we would be?

Leaders who realize they've drifted from their core values face a crucial choice: continue the self-deception or embrace the painful truth as the first step toward authenticity. This moment of reckoning isn't just personal; it can transform organizations, creating cultures of genuine integrity rather than just compliance.

I discovered that what I thought was protecting me had actually been constraining me. The perfect image wasn't a shield; it was a self-imposed prison made of glass walls. This shedding continues to be a daily practice. The armor doesn't disappear overnight; it has a way of creeping back when we're stressed, threatened, or uncertain. But now I recognize it for what it is, a reaction to fear rather than a source of strength.

Today, when I speak to organizations about authentic leadership, I often begin by asking executives to identify their own armor. What parts of themselves do they believe are too messy, too complicated, too vulnerable to bring into professional spaces? How much energy are they expending to maintain separate personas across contexts? What fears drive their need for perfect control?

These questions often spark profound realizations. Leaders begin to see how their armor limits their impact, restricts their connections, and depletes their energy. They start to imagine what might be possible if they redirected that energy toward innovation, collaboration, and genuine presence.

The liberation comes not from abandoning standards or accountability but from releasing the exhausting performance of perfection. It comes from understanding that our humanity, with all its complexity, struggle, and imperfection, is not a liability to overcome but the very source of our leadership power.

The journey of shedding armor isn't about lowering standards or abandoning excellence. It's about recognizing that our greatest strength comes not from projecting perfection but from embracing our humanity. Not from hiding our struggles but from transforming them into bridges of connection and catalysts for growth.

Each piece of armor I shed—the perfectionism, the performance, the people-pleasing—removed another part of the frame I had hidden behind. The more I released these protective layers, the more clearly I could see how exhausting it had been to maintain the perfect picture.

The armor that I thought protected me had actually been the gilded frame that kept me from truly living in the moment, from being authentically present in my own life.

In the space of surrender, something unexpected happened. As each piece of armor fell away, I didn't feel more vulnerable; I felt lighter. The energy I had been pouring into maintaining these protective layers was suddenly available for growth, for connection, for presence.

LEADERSHIP LESSONS: SHEDDING THE ARMOR

1. **Recognize our imperfections.** Pretending to be flawless drains our energy and isolates us. When we acknowledge our imperfections, we free ourselves, and our teams, to innovate, connect, and grow.
2. **Own our true selves.** Power doesn't come from perfecting our image; it comes from showing up real. When leaders embrace their full selves, they create cultures where authenticity fuels performance.
3. **Shame thrives in silence.** The more we hide our struggles, the more power they hold over us. When leaders create environments where it's safe to speak honestly about challenges, real progress begins.
4. **Authentic leadership begins when we stop performing and start living our values.** Leadership rooted in performance is fragile. Leadership rooted in lived values is transformative and fosters trust, resilience, and lasting impact.

REFLECTION QUESTIONS

- Where am I spending energy trying to appear perfect instead of focusing on what truly matters?
- How could bringing more of my full self to work strengthen my leadership and my relationships?
- What struggles or doubts have I been keeping hidden out of fear or shame?

CHAPTER 10

Breaking Open, Rising Through

CONTROL IS AN ILLUSION

October 2007: I sat across from the operations director in his glass and chrome conference room, trying not to show how desperately I needed this client. The North Miami Beach view shimmered beyond the windows, a perfect backdrop for success.

"So there is a third-party disbursement on the settlement statement?" I asked, already sensing something wasn't quite right.

"Yes, it's all standard," he assured me, sliding another document across the desk. "Many developers are doing this now. It's how we move inventory in this market." He told me that he had been working for a few years on these transactions with another big law firm. We talked about a rental guarantee and a trust to which the money would be disbursed.

I nodded, pushing down the discomfort rising in my stomach. I saw red flags. I knew. But I didn't stop. I didn't want to.

During the meeting, I called my title insurance underwriter, explaining the transactions but, here's where it gets complicated, not fully. I emphasized the parts that would gain approval while minimizing elements that might raise concerns.

"The third-party disbursement will be shown on the settlement statement," I explained. What I didn't mention was the financial benefit flowing to the buyers.

I didn't give all the facts because I was desperate. I see that now. That's the hardest truth.

I wasn't lying, I told myself. I was just focusing on the relevant parts. But the omission was as dishonest as any lie.

Control is an illusion. Desperation distorts discernment. I had been gripping so tightly to my need for this client, to my image of success, to my financial stability that I'd closed myself off from the warning signals flashing all around me. When we're desperate, we lose perspective. We see only what we want to see, hear only what we need to hear. Desperation makes us deaf to wisdom and blind to consequences.

The irony wasn't lost on me; in my desperate attempt to control my financial future, I was surrendering control of my ethical judgment. Each compromise felt necessary in the moment, justified by the pressure to succeed, to provide, to maintain the lifestyle that had become my identity.

The closings began to be consistent. The volume was staggering, the complexity challenging. I threw myself into creating perfect systems, flawless documentation. My staff expanded. Revenue grew. Finally, I was achieving at the level I'd been groomed for all my life.

But there were moments, small, quiet moments, when something felt off. A realtor would make a comment about payments happening outside closing. A buyer would seem confused about the rental guarantee structure. Each time, I would push away the doubt and focus on the documentation, on keeping my files perfect.

One time, I even got an email from another developer's attorney (who I was trying to convince to use me as his title attorney) warning me, in no uncertain words, that he thought these transactions could amount to fraud. But I didn't listen. I filed the email away and ignored it. I didn't even call him to discuss it. I thought to myself, *He is an old-timer. I am being strategic and aggressive; I am thinking outside the box and being creative.*

LETTING GO IS A POWER MOVE

Boy, do I wish I could go back and relive that day. I wish I would have picked up the phone and sought his advice. I was arrogant and caught in ego.

Perfectionism became a mask. Arrogance became a shield. The more perfect my files appeared, the more I could convince myself that everything was legitimate. The more successful I became, the more I believed my own narrative of innovation and strategic thinking. Perfectionism wasn't about excellence; it was about avoiding the uncomfortable questions that threatened my carefully constructed reality.

Arrogance whispered that I was smarter than the "old-timers," that I was pioneering new approaches they were too conservative to understand. But arrogance is just fear wearing a confident mask, fear that I wasn't as competent as I needed to be, fear that I didn't belong in the success I was trying so hard to maintain.

I had seen the red flags. I chose not to look. That was my choice.

When I finally made the decision to plead guilty, something shifted inside me. Pleading guilty wasn't just a legal decision; it was about finally being honest with myself. It wasn't just a strategic move to reduce my sentence; it was an act of reclaiming my integrity.

In the legal profession, we're trained to spot issues, identify problems, and ask tough questions. Yet when it came to my own practice and my own financial security, I had suspended that training. I had turned off the professional judgment I had spent years developing.

This realization was perhaps the most painful of all, that I had failed not just legally but professionally. That I had betrayed not just the law but the oath I had taken as an attorney.

SUCCESS SOMETIMES REQUIRES SUBTRACTION

Success isn't about doing more; it's about subtracting what no longer serves. For years, I'd been adding: more clients, more cases, more hours, more achievements. But real growth began only when I started subtracting, removing the layers of denial, the desperate performance, the mask of perfectionism that had become my prison.

The weight of these realizations nearly crushed me. There were days I couldn't get out of bed, nights I couldn't sleep. The shame was a physical presence, a heaviness in my chest that made it hard to breathe.

Yet something else was happening, too, something I couldn't yet name or fully understand. In the space created by my surrender to the truth, new insights began to emerge. I started to see patterns in my behavior that had been invisible to me before, how I had always prioritized achievement over alignment, how I had measured my worth by external markers, how I had confused success with integrity.

The moment of sentencing became the ultimate breaking open, not just of my circumstances but of every carefully constructed layer I had built around myself. At sentencing, I wept uncontrollably. The perfect child had fallen. And something deeper rose.

This wasn't just emotional release; it was complete surrender to reality. Every mask I had worn, every performance I had maintained, every illusion of control I had clung to, all of it dissolved in that instant. The facade was gone. The performance was over. All that remained was the raw, real person beneath the mask.

I had fallen, yes. But in that falling, I was also, paradoxically, rising.

In the midst of this painful reckoning, unexpected grace appeared. When I finally broke down and told other parents at my children's school what was happening, they organized meal deliveries for my family. When I confessed to old friends from college, they sent letters of support to the judge. When I shared the truth with my extended family, they surrounded me with love rather than judgment.

I had expected rejection. I had expected to be cast out, to be seen as a disgrace. Instead, I was met with compassion. Not because what I had done was acceptable, it wasn't, but because the people who truly knew me could hold both truths: that I had made serious mistakes and that I was more than those mistakes.

This taught me something profound about surrender, that it opens doors we cannot open through force. When I finally let go of the desperate need to defend and justify myself, when I simply stood in the truth of what had happened, I created space for connections I hadn't known were possible.

STILLNESS CREATES STRATEGY

Surrender is not weakness; it's the birthplace of transformation. In the stillness after my collapse, after the frantic denial and defense had ceased, I could finally hear the quiet voice of wisdom within me. I could see more clearly what mattered, what didn't, and how I wanted to move forward.

During the two months between my sentencing and my surrender date, I had time to reflect on the journey that had brought me to this point. I thought about the patterns that had shaped my choices, my lifelong drive for achievement, my need for approval, my fear of disappointing others.

I thought about the email I had received that Christmas Eve, the one about the rental guarantee. I had known, somewhere deep down, that something wasn't right. But instead of investigating, instead of asking questions, I had forwarded it to my staff and gone back to my holiday celebrations. I had chosen convenience over conscience, comfort over courage.

These reflections weren't about self-flagellation. They were about understanding the mechanics of my fall so that I could build differently next time. They were about seeing clearly the patterns that had led me to this point so that I could choose different patterns going forward.

I began to see surrender not as weakness but as wisdom, the wisdom to know when fighting is futile, when resistance is costing more than it's worth, when letting go is the path to growth rather than defeat.

By the time I arrived at Coleman Federal Prison Camp, I had already spent ten days at the Federal Detention Center in Miami, ten days that felt like a lifetime. The transport to Coleman had been dehumanizing: chained at the waist, wrists, and ankles, then loaded onto a bus with other women for the hours-long journey.

But Coleman was different from the detention center. Here, there were no cells, just open dormitories with bunk beds. There was a track where I could run. There was a sense, however constrained, of community. After the concrete and steel of Miami, Coleman felt almost pastoral with its grass and trees, though the guards reminded you that freedom was still an illusion.

The bright Florida sun beat down on Coleman as I walked the track for the first time. Three weeks had passed since my surrender, and I was finally settling into a rhythm, though not one I had ever imagined for myself. The shell-covered track crunched beneath my prison-issued sneakers, a far cry from the cushioned running paths of Pinecrest where I had logged thousands of miles in my previous life.

This morning, like every morning, I counted my steps. Three laps equaled one mile, 1,800 steps exactly. I had always been methodical, a planner, someone who needed control. Now, in a place where control was systematically taken away, I clung to what little I could manage: my step count, my running schedule, the small rituals I was building day by day.

The stripping away had begun the moment I surrendered, not just the literal stripping during processing but the systematic removal of everything that had defined me. My law license was already gone.

My professional identity had evaporated. My carefully constructed image as the perfect immigrant daughter, the successful attorney, the community leader, all of it had crumbled the moment the judge pronounced my sentence.

Now, wearing a prison uniform with ID number 05121-104 always on my pocket, I was learning what remained when everything external was taken away. The question that haunted my early days at Coleman wasn't "How will I survive this?" but rather "Who am I when I'm not performing for anyone?"

At Coleman, every inmate was assigned a job. My first job assignment was "compound trash." Every evening, just before recall (when all inmates must return to their housing units), I would collect the large trash bins from beside each housing unit and wheel them to the back of the complex, behind the dining hall. There, I would empty each bag into the compactor, making sure nothing fell to the ground.

The irony was not lost on me. Less than a year ago, I had been reviewing complex legal documents in climate-controlled offices, attended by staff who handled every detail of my professional life. Now I was being handed work gloves and instructed on the proper technique for emptying garbage bins.

This was no clean or simple task. Often the bags would burst open as I tried to hoist them into the compactor. When this happened, I would have to use the gloves they had given me to fish out the garbage from the bottom of the huge bins and place it piece by piece into the compactor. It was messy, smelly work, about as far from the pristine environment of a law office as one could imagine.

For the first few weeks, I tried to time my trash runs when I thought fewer people would be around. I didn't want to be seen pushing garbage bins, didn't want my "fall" to be so visible. I imagined everyone was watching me, judging me, whispering about the fallen lawyer now handling their trash.

Then one evening, my bunkie Michelle said something that shifted my perspective: "Nobody's watching you, Rashmi. Everyone here is just trying to survive their own story."

She was right. The women sitting outside their units weren't gossiping about me; they were lost in their own thoughts, missing their own children, fighting their own battles. My shame about pushing trash bins was just another form of ego, another way of thinking I was somehow different or special.

EMBRACE CURIOSITY AND LET GO OF JUDGMENT

Let go of judgment; embrace curiosity. I had arrived at Coleman so certain about who I was, a successful attorney temporarily derailed by a mistake. This certainty was both a shield and a prison. It kept me separate from the women around me, reinforcing a hierarchy that existed only in my mind.

As the weeks passed, my certainty began to crack. I watched women I might have previously dismissed demonstrate incredible resilience, creativity, and wisdom. I saw how my rigid categorizations, of myself and others, limited what I could learn and who I could become.

As I released my judgment about trash duty, and about so many other aspects of prison life, I became more curious. What brought each woman to Coleman? What could I learn from this experience that might serve me later?

This shift from judgment to curiosity transformed my prison experience. Instead of seeing my circumstances as a punishment to be endured, I began to approach them as a classroom for deeper wisdom. My question changed from "Why is this happening to me?" to "What is this teaching me?"

GRACE TRANSFORMS TEAMS

Growth lives in the in-between. Grace is a leadership differentiator. This truth revealed itself to me slowly during those early weeks at Coleman. I had spent my entire life categorizing things as success or failure, right or wrong, good or bad. But prison stripped away these neat categories, forcing me to navigate the murky middle where most of life actually happens.

My crime itself lived in this gray area. I hadn't set out to commit fraud. There was no moment when I decided to cross a clear ethical line. Instead, there were a series of small compromises, rationalizations, and blind spots that accumulated over time. Understanding this complexity didn't excuse my actions, but it helped me develop a more nuanced view of human behavior, both my own and others'.

Perhaps the most profound lesson of my prison experience was learning to extend grace to myself and to others. Grace isn't about excusing wrongdoing or ignoring accountability. It's about recognizing our shared humanity, our capacity for both terrible mistakes and extraordinary redemption.

This lesson came to me gradually, through the daily practice of accepting my circumstances and finding meaning within them. When a bag of trash burst open as I was loading it into the compactor, covering my shoes with bathroom and food waste, I could choose anger and disgust or acceptance and humor. When another woman was rude or dismissive, I could respond with judgment or with understanding that her behavior likely reflected her own struggle.

Patricia, "Mom" to everyone in our unit, became an unexpected mentor in this process. A former office manager for a law firm serving time for wire fraud committed by her bosses, she had transformed her own pain into a mission of mothering everyone around her.

"Perfection is a prison," she told me one evening as we sat crocheting together. "And you've been in that one far longer than you'll be in this one."

Her words struck deep. The perfect child, the straight-A student, the high-achieving professional, these identities had indeed been prisons of their own. They had kept me striving endlessly, never feeling like I was enough, always needing to prove my worth through achievement.

This acceptance extended to my relationships, particularly with my children. During visits, I stopped trying to present a perfect facade. I allowed them to see my authentic emotions, my joy at seeing them, my sadness at our separation, my hope for our future reunion. These more honest exchanges deepened our connection in ways I hadn't expected.

With each passing week, I let go of the version of me who needed approval, status, and a perfect image, and embraced who I was becoming. This wasn't about abandoning ambition or excellence. It was about redefining them in more authentic, more sustainable ways.

I began to offer myself grace.

Almost six months into my sentence at Coleman anand after I had testified in the other case in Tampa, Joe, my prosecutor, filed a Rule

35 motion, a request for the judge to reduce my sentence based on my substantial assistance in the Tampa case. It was rare for prosecutors to file such motions, and I tried not to get my hopes up.

The hearing was scheduled for 9:00 a.m. on a Friday. I had been told to call David at 10:00 a.m., as he would know the outcome by then. Standing at the pay phone in my housing unit, I punched in all the required numbers to make the call. As soon as the connection went through, David's voice exploded through the receiver:

"YOU'RE GOING HOME!"

I couldn't believe it. After months of surrender, of accepting my circumstances, of finding meaning in confinement, suddenly, freedom was within reach. My hands shook as I called my parents next.

"Mom, the judge granted the motion. I'm coming home today. Can Dad leave now to come get me?"

There was a pause, then my mother's joyful exclamation: "Honey, your father left an hour ago!" That's the kind of faith my parents have. Even before knowing the outcome, my parents had believed. They had acted on hope.

I had made chocolate truffles for my children the day before, hoping against hope that I might be coming home early. Now I gave away all my belongings—clothes, food, toiletries—to the women who had become my community. I packed up my few remaining possessions and got all the required paperwork signed by the guards.

Then came the waiting. Even though the judge had ruled at the 9:00 a.m. hearing, the order had to be prepared and sent to the warden at my prison. The Bureau of Prisons had to acknowledge it before I could be released. Hours passed. I sat in receiving and discharge, no longer an inmate but not yet free.

When I finally got in the car with my father, I held my phone for the first time in six months. It felt odd and heavy in my hands; this device that had once been an extension of my body now felt foreign. We stopped at the first turnpike rest stop so I could change out of my prison clothes. My mother had sent fresh clothes for me to change into.

I had asked my parents not to tell the children, wanting to surprise them. When we arrived home, my mother performed a small puja outside to welcome me back, a ritual of gratitude and blessing. Then I ran inside the house.

My kids enveloped me in their arms and didn't let go. Kyler and Maya held me so tightly, as if they could prevent me from ever leaving again. In that moment, surrounded by their love, something crystallized with perfect clarity.

This is what my life is for. To be present for them. To become the best version of myself for them. To grow and be honest and hold myself accountable for them. To impact the world and create my legacy for them.

The breaking open that had begun with my collapse outside the temple, that had continued through my plea and sentencing, reached its completion in that embrace. I had lost everything I thought defined me—my career, my reputation, my freedom—only to discover what actually mattered. Not achievement or appearance, but presence. Not perfection, but authenticity. Not success as the world measures it, but love as only family can give it.

The Rule 35 hearing wasn't just about legal mercy; it was about the completion of a transformation. I had surrendered everything, accepted the consequences of my choices, and found grace on the other side. Not because I deserved it but because surrender had opened me to receive it.

The perfect child who once chased achievement at any cost was transforming into a woman who understood that true success isn't in avoiding falls but in rising through them with grace and purpose. The attorney who once built walls of credentials was becoming someone who built bridges of authentic connection. The mother who was physically present but emotionally absent was evolving into someone who could be fully present, even from a distance.

Stripped of everything external, I finally confronted what remained within the frame, not the perfect image I had projected but the raw, real person I actually was. Without my designer clothes, my prestigious title, my carefully constructed narrative, what was left?

I discovered that when there's nothing left to hide behind, you find what's real. And that reality—messy, imperfect, authentic—was far more valuable than the polished picture I had been so desperate to maintain. In losing my freedom, I gained total freedom.

In the stripping away, we find what's real. We find grace. And what's real—our core values, our authentic voice, our capacity for growth and connection—is the foundation upon which truly transformative leadership is built.

Breaking open isn't the end. It's the beginning.

LEADERSHIP LESSONS: BREAKING OPEN, RISING THROUGH

1. **Control is an illusion.** The tighter you grip, the more you lose perspective and possibility.
2. **Letting go is a power move.** Surrender allows you to receive what force never can.

3. **Success sometimes requires subtraction.** Eliminate the masks, the ego, the noise.
4. **Grace transforms teams.** Extend it to yourself and others to create safety and innovation.

REFLECTION QUESTIONS:

- What truth are you resisting that your gut already knows?
- How do you define success, and what needs to be subtracted to live that truth?
- In what situation can you shift from judgment to curiosity?

Prison Hack

PRISON CHOCOLATE TRUFFLES

INGREDIENTS:

- 2 packs chocolate cookies (Oreos)
- 4 oz cream cheese
- 1 stick butter
- 4 tbs powdered creamer
- 8 oz chocolate milk
- 2 Hershey bars

PROCESS:

1. Crush cookies and mix all dry ingredients.
2. Combine butter, creamer, and cream cheese, soften slightly in microwave, then add to powdered mixture.
3. Slowly add milk until mixture is firm enough to be shaped into balls.
4. Roll dough into balls with 1" diameter.
5. Break up Hershey bars and melt in microwave in 5-second intervals, stirring in between. Do not overheat.
6. Once chocolate is melted, roll balls in chocolate and place on wax paper and allow to cool completely.
7. Enjoy delicious truffles.

PART 4

Evolve

Evolving isn't about returning to who we were before challenges changed us; it's about becoming who we were meant to be because of them. The final pillar of the RISE Framework focuses on intentional transformation: integrating our experiences, wisdom, and purpose into a more authentic expression of leadership. These chapters reveal that evolution isn't a destination but a continuous practice of becoming more aligned with our deepest truths.

This evolution requires both intention and attention, the disciplined commitment to daily practices that build new neural pathways and leadership habits. It's not about perfection but integration; it's not about abandoning our past but weaving it into a more textured, purposeful present. The most impactful leaders don't just know different things; they embody different ways of being in the world.

When I emerged from prison, I discovered that my greatest

contribution wouldn't come from recreating my former life but from evolving into a more purposeful expression of service. The chapters ahead demonstrate how presence becomes more powerful than performance, how healed wounds transform into unique wisdom, and how authentic leadership creates ripples that extend far beyond our individual stories. Evolution isn't just about personal growth; it's about creating a legacy impact that serves something larger than ourselves.

CHAPTER 11

Learning, Unlearning, and Growing

As I stood in the prison yard watching the sunrise one morning, I realized something profound. Evolution isn't just about adding more; it's about letting go of what no longer serves us. It's about releasing the limiting beliefs, the destructive patterns, and the false identities that keep us small.

EVOLUTION IS A CHOICE, NOT A CHANCE

For me, this meant letting go of some deeply ingrained patterns: the belief that my worth was tied to achievement, the relentless need to appear perfect at all costs, the habit of defining success by external metrics, and the fear that vulnerability would somehow diminish my leadership. These mindsets had shaped much of my life, but over time, I realized they were barriers rather than bridges, keeping me locked in cycles of performance and approval rather than genuine growth and connection.

In their place, I began to embrace a new foundation: recognizing my intrinsic worth, independent of any performance or accolade; showing up with authentic presence instead of chasing a perfect image; redefining success through the lens of impact, integrity, and alignment with my values; and understanding vulnerability not as a weakness but as a profound source of connection and influence.

This shift wasn't easy, but it opened the door to a deeper, more purposeful way of leading and living.

The morning after my release from prison, I woke up disoriented. The mattress felt too soft, the darkness too complete without the constant institutional lighting I'd grown accustomed to. For a moment, I couldn't place where I was. Then I felt a small hand on my arm; Maya had crawled into bed beside me sometime during the night. The world suddenly snapped back into focus.

"Mommy, are you really staying home forever now?" she whispered, her voice tiny in the predawn stillness.

"Yes, baby. I'm home for good."

But as the days unfolded, I realized that while I had physically returned, I was not the same woman who had left. Prison hadn't just been something that happened to me; it had transformed me.

The question was: How would I use that transformation?

Evolution is a choice.

Every leader reaches a moment where they must choose discomfort over default, truth over tradition. For my father, that choice came when he decided to pursue higher education and later apply to graduate schools in America. For many leaders, it comes in similarly pivotal moments, when continuing along the established path feels safer, but transformation calls for a different direction entirely.

BREAK THE CYCLE OR REPEAT IT

One of the most powerful examples of my parents' evolutionary leadership was how they approached cultural traditions. Rather than blindly following customs, they questioned, examined, and thoughtfully decided which to preserve and which to transform.

The tradition of dowry, where a bride's family gives goods, cash, or property to the groom's family, was deeply embedded in Indian culture. Though officially illegal, many families still found ways to honor or disguise it. My father made a quiet but radical statement when he refused dowry at his marriage to my mother, accepting only a single symbolic rupee to honor tradition while rejecting its harmful premise.

That simple gesture carried profound meaning. It said that my mother was not a commodity, that marriage was a partnership built on respect, not transaction. It also showed me what true courage looks like, not loud defiance but the steady willingness to live your values even when the world disagrees.

Breaking cycles is not easy. It demands self-awareness and conviction. Legacy leadership is born when you interrupt unconscious patterns in yourself, your company, or your culture. My father did not simply disagree with dowry practices in private; he took a public stand at a time when few dared to. In doing so, he broke a generational cycle of silence and complicity.

This same courage guided him years later when we moved to Miami. Many immigrant families found safety in cultural enclaves, clinging to the familiarity of their own community. But my father believed that comfort could become confinement. He joined the Rotary Club, became active in local politics, and built genuine friendships across racial and cultural lines. He never abandoned his Indian identity, but he refused to let it become a barrier to connection or contribution.

He modeled this principle again when he started his engineering firm. In the construction and infrastructure world, paying referral fees or bribes to secure government contracts was considered normal. My father refused. He would not bend his ethics for convenience or profit.

When an official from the town of Surfside asked for a $2,000 payment to approve a project, my father did something extraordinary. He reported the request to the authorities, agreed to cooperate with the state attorney's office, and wore a wire to expose the corruption. He carried marked bills into a meeting to help secure the evidence that led to the official's arrest and conviction.

Later, when I asked him why he went through such an ordeal, he smiled and said, "Instead of paying a $2,000 bribe, I spent 2,000 hours helping get him convicted." That experience transformed him. It inspired him to go to law school, adding a new layer of knowledge to his engineering background so he could better navigate and influence the systems he worked within.

The temple project revealed yet another side of my parents' leadership. When they became financially successful in the 1980s, they did not focus solely on building personal wealth. They invested their time, energy, and resources in creating something larger than themselves.

My father recognized that the growing Indian community in South Florida needed a cultural and spiritual anchor, a place where families could gather, worship, and feel a sense of belonging.

Rather than waiting for someone else to act, he and a group of friends identified land for the first Hindu Temple of South Florida. They formed a committee, raised funds, overcame zoning hurdles, and guided every step of construction. What they built was more than a structure of stone and wood. It was a symbol of faith, identity, and community resilience.

Their choices taught me that real leadership is not about dominance or control. It is about conscious evolution, about taking the traditions and lessons of the past and reshaping them to serve a higher purpose.

My parents' actions were not just about what they stood against but what they stood for: equality, integrity, belonging, and courage.

DON'T OUTSOURCE YOUR AUTHORITY

Stop waiting for someone else to change the system. Choose to lead from within or beyond it.

My parents never waited for someone else to build what they believed in. They didn't delegate responsibility for community building; they stepped forward and acted themselves. Real change rarely begins in a conference room. It begins when someone decides to take personal responsibility for what needs to be done.

This philosophy guided every part of their lives. They didn't pursue leadership positions for status or recognition but to make something meaningful happen. My mother served on nonprofit boards dedicated to women's empowerment and taught classes at a local college, giving generously of her time and expertise without expectation of return. My father offered pro bono engineering services to underserved communities, using his skills to improve lives rather than simply advance his career.

For both, education was never about collecting degrees or accolades. It was about transformation. In the 1980s, when most people would have settled comfortably into established careers, they made the bold decision to attend law school at night while running their business during the day. My father went first, and then, in a moment that perfectly captures their partnership, he convinced my mother to enroll as his birthday gift.

It was not an easy path. They worked long hours, studied late into the night, and balanced parenting with relentless determination. They didn't need law degrees to maintain their business, but they understood that expanding their knowledge would open new possibilities and deepen their capacity to serve others.

After graduating, they didn't abandon their previous expertise. They built upon it. My father combined his engineering and real estate experience with real estate law, while my mother merged her background in economics with estate planning. Together, they developed a multidimensional practice that reflected their belief in lifelong learning and integrated leadership.

Their example taught me that mastery isn't a destination but a continual process of growth. The real leaders are those who keep learning long after they could stop, who keep evolving long after success might have made them complacent. They rise not by chasing titles but by expanding their impact through curiosity, courage, and commitment to serve.

EVOLUTION ISN'T EASY

My parents taught me that education never ends. It is not confined to classrooms or credentials but is a lifelong commitment to growth and expansion. This principle has guided my own evolution from lawyer to prisoner to purpose-driven leader. Each stage demanded new learning, new understanding, and the courage to integrate rather than separate each experience.

Perhaps the most profound transformation I witnessed in my parents was their shift from pursuing success to embodying service. In the beginning, like many immigrants, they focused on stability and creating opportunities for their children. Service mattered, but survival came first. As they became more secure, something in them evolved. They began to see their accomplishments not as the goal but as a foundation for contribution.

When my sister Catherine was diagnosed with a mental health condition, everything changed again. The diagnosis forced our family to face the painful gaps in the mental health system. My parents responded the only way they knew how, with love, action, and purpose. They volunteered, advocated, and built support networks for families like ours, especially those in multicultural communities. Their work eventually led to the co-founding of Key Clubhouse of South Florida, a community that provides belonging and structure for people living with mental illness.

Their journey from personal ambition to public service to systemic impact became a model for my own growth. When my world fell apart, when I lost my career, my reputation, and my freedom, I believed my life was over. But their example showed me that evolution is not destroyed by loss; it begins there.

In prison, I created small rituals that anchored me. I ran at dawn to quiet my mind. I taught math to women who had never been told they were intelligent. I wrote morning reflections and evening gratitude lists. I learned to crochet from a woman who taught me that creation itself can be a form of healing. Each act, no matter how small, became a building block of transformation. It was not a sudden rebirth but a slow, steady process of becoming more aligned with truth.

After my release, that evolution deepened. I had to rebuild not only my career but my understanding of who I was. This work extended into my marriage to Erik. Despite our efforts, we could not repair the distance that my choices and years of emotional absence had created. Our marriage ended, and I accept full responsibility for my part in that outcome: the misplaced priorities, the chronic performing, the way I valued achievement over presence.

Even in that loss, growth continued. Erik and I redefined our relationship with compassion to a solid friendship. We have built a strong and loving partnership as co-parents. His grace and unwavering commitment to our children continue to humble me. Together, we learned to honor what we built while giving each other the freedom to evolve into our truest selves. Like my parents before me, I realized that real impact comes not from preserving old forms but from transforming experience into purpose.

Today, my work with leaders centers on this same truth. Real evolution is not about escaping struggle or reinventing ourselves to look stronger. It is about allowing challenge to reveal what must grow. It is about shifting from control to creation, from perfection to presence, from image to integrity. I help leaders see disruption not as a crisis to survive but as an invitation to evolve.

Evolution is not a destination. It is a daily practice of becoming, because we never "arrive." Do we?

Some days, I still catch myself reaching for old habits of perfectionism or fear, but I notice it now. I pause, breathe, and choose differently.

The greatest gift my parents gave me was not comfort or success but their living example of how to rise through hardship with dignity and faith. From my father, I learned that learning itself is liberation. From my mother, I learned that vision and strategy can turn pain into purpose. From both, I learned that integrity, not perfection, is the truest measure of success.

Evolution asks us to stop rebuilding what has broken and to imagine what can be created instead. It is not about restoring an old frame but about reimagining what belongs inside it. Success and failure, joy and grief, strength and vulnerability all have a rightful place within a life that is fully lived.

When I look back at my journey, from the perfectionist achiever to the woman stripped of everything to the leader guided by purpose, I see not a straight line but a vortex. Each fall brought me closer to truth. Each loss expanded my capacity for compassion and clarity.

This is evolution in its purest form, raw and honest and deeply human. The woman who once chased validation now stands rooted in truth. The leader who once performed certainty now embodies courage. The mother who once measured worth by achievement now builds legacy through love.

Evolution does not wait for ideal conditions. It rises from the very places we thought would destroy us. It transforms our deepest wounds into our greatest sources of wisdom. It is not reinvention. It is reclamation. It is the ongoing evolution of becoming who we were always meant to be.

LEADERSHIP LESSONS: LEARNING, UNLEARNING, AND GROWING

1. **Evolution is a choice, not a chance.** Every leader reaches a moment where they must choose discomfort over default, truth over tradition. I chose authenticity over appearance. What will you choose?
2. **Break the cycle or repeat it.** Legacy leadership is born when you interrupt unconscious patterns, in yourself, in your company, in your culture. I broke patterns of perfectionism and performance. What cycles are you perpetuating? What patterns could you break?
3. **Don't outsource your authority.** Stop waiting for someone else to change the system. Choose to lead from within or beyond it. I didn't wait for someone else to extract meaning from my fall. In what ways are you waiting for permission instead of taking action?
4. **Evolution isn't easy.** It requires us to face uncomfortable truths, release familiar identities, and step into uncertainty without guarantees. But in that evolution lies the potential for impact beyond anything we could achieve through mere success. The question isn't whether you'll face moments that challenge your identity, your beliefs, and your sense of what's possible; it's whether you'll use those moments to evolve.

REFLECTION QUESTIONS

- Where do you need to create more pause in your life? What decisions or interactions would benefit from more intentional presence?
- What cycles (personal, organizational, or cultural) are you unconsciously perpetuating? What would it look like to break them?
- Think of a crisis or setback you've faced. How did it force you to evolve? What did you learn to let go of, and what did you embrace instead?

CHAPTER 12

Rising into My Purpose

Years have passed since I came home from prison. Morning light filters through my kitchen window, soft and golden, landing on the rising steam from my coffee. I pause, hands wrapped around the mug, feeling the warmth spread through me. From where I stand, I can see the blankets I crocheted in prison draped across the couch. They are imperfect but beautiful, woven with surrender, hope, and love. They remind me of who I became when everything else was stripped away.

About five years after I came home, I made the decision to move in with my parents. At first, it was purely practical. Finances were tight, and continuing to live on my own no longer made sense. But what began as a decision born of necessity has become one of the greatest blessings of my life. Living with them again has given me the rare chance to know them not just as my parents but as people, real, complex, beautifully human. I get to share morning tea with my mother, to hear my father's voice during his prayers, to sit at the table where so much of my life was shaped and now see it from a new perspective. What I once feared would feel like regression has become renewal. I would not trade this season for anything.

The house is peaceful now, filled with the soft sounds of everyday life, the low hum of the refrigerator, my mother moving around the kitchen, my father's quiet chanting of mantras from his room. This is the calm before the movement. Later today, I will fly to Dallas to speak to hundreds of executives about authentic leadership and rising through adversity. But before any of that, I do what centers me most. I check in with Maya and Kyler.

Maya sends me a blurry Snapchat, her hair tousled, her face still half buried in her pillow. "Morning, Posh," she writes, using the nickname that began as Rashmi, then Rosh Posh, and somehow became Posh. It stuck, and now all her friends call me that too. I love it. She is in college now, with a heart that radiates kindness and empathy. She is pure and grounded, both fierce and tender. Her compassion is effortless, and she reminds me daily that strength can be soft.

Kyler calls a few minutes later. His voice is bright, brimming with purpose. He tells me about his classes, fraternity meetings, and campus leadership projects. He pushes himself the way I once did, chasing goals with tireless focus. My mini me. I listen with pride and with the quiet ache of recognition. I want to pull him close, to hold his face in my hands, and tell him that he is already enough, that his value is not in the doing but in the being. I tell him often, but I know he will have to find that truth in his own way, just as I did.

These small moments with my children are sacred. They remind me that connection is not measured by proximity but by presence. That love does not require achievement. That showing up again and again with honesty and grace is enough.

Evolution is not a finish line. It is a daily practice of choosing truth over image, presence over performance, and wholeness over perfection. The path is not straight. It circles back on itself, returning me to lessons I thought I had mastered, each time with deeper understanding.

When I first came home, I believed my transformation was complete. I thought the hardest part was behind me. But the real work began in the small, ordinary choices. When I said no to something I did not need to prove. When I spoke my truth without filtering out the pain. When I felt the pull of perfectionism and chose authenticity instead.

Transformation does not live in grand moments or on stages. It lives here, in the soft hum of a shared home, in Maya's sleepy face on a screen, in Kyler's confident but searching voice, in my parents' laughter echoing down the hallway. It lives in the quiet rhythm of ordinary mornings, in the daily decision to keep rising, to keep loving, and to keep becoming.

THE HEALED SELF LEADS DIFFERENTLY

Walking onto the stage at the leadership conference in Dallas, I feel an unfamiliar stillness inside me. For years, I carried the weight of proving myself, the invisible armor of credentials and accomplishments that I thought made me worthy of being seen. Now, I walk with nothing to prove and nothing to hide. The applause washes over me, but it no longer defines me. What fills me instead is peace, the quiet knowing that I am enough simply as I am. This is what freedom feels like, not the absence of struggle, but the release of needing to perform. It is the most profound shift in how I show up as a human being, not built on titles or triumphs, but on truth.

I had to lose my freedom to gain complete freedom.

The greatest paradox of my life is that prison became the place where I found liberation. Stripped of everything that once defined me, I discovered the freedom that comes from no longer needing to perform, prove, or please. The woman who once measured her worth through success now walks in quiet conviction.

Your healed self leads differently. No longer hustling for validation or hiding behind titles, you lead with conviction and clarity born from experience. Healing reshapes not only how you live but how you lead.

I see this contrast clearly when I work with executives. Those still carrying unhealed shame or self-doubt often lead reactively, from fear rather than wisdom. They control outcomes, avoid vulnerability, and protect their image at all costs. Their leadership mirrors their inner landscape: rigid, defensive, and performance driven.

The healed leader moves differently. Not because they have avoided struggle but because they have faced it and done the inner work those struggles demanded. They have learned to integrate their pain rather than deny it.

Before prison, I led from a place of proving. I needed to be the smartest, most prepared, most impressive person in every room. My worth was tethered to achievement, my identity built on how others saw me. I confused control with strength and perfection with value. My leadership looked polished from the outside but was rooted in fear.

Today, I lead from a deeper well of self-knowledge and acceptance. I am not afraid of difficult conversations because I have had the hardest one with myself. I am not threatened by others' success because I no longer measure my worth through comparison. I am not paralyzed by the fear of mistakes because I have lived through failure and learned that my strength was never in avoiding pain but in rising through it.

This healed version of leadership reveals itself in small, quiet moments that carry enormous weight. The courage to say, "I don't know" when I truly don't. The strength to make decisions without chasing approval. The wisdom to choose integrity over image. The calm to hold space when everything around me feels uncertain. The clarity to remember that my worth and my work are not the same thing.

This is not abstract theory. It is a lived transformation I now witness in others. When leaders begin to heal their own wounds rather than projecting them onto their teams, entire cultures shift. Trust deepens. Communication opens. Creativity expands. People feel safe to bring their whole selves to work because they see it modeled by the person in charge.

The most powerful leadership development does not happen in boardrooms or workshops. It happens in quiet moments of truth, when leaders face their own reflection, acknowledge their blind spots, and choose to lead with honesty rather than ego. That is where the real transformation begins.

INTEGRATION, NOT PERFECTION

I'm no longer trying to fit into a predetermined frame or create the perfect picture for others to admire. Instead, I'm fully present in the frame of my life, experiencing it rather than just appearing in it. The frame has transformed from a confining border into a window through which I both receive and offer authentic connection. This isn't about crafting an impressive image anymore; it's about living a genuinely impactful life, one where I'm no longer performing for the frame but truly present within it.

In business contexts, we often operate as if transformation requires abandoning everything that came before. The struggling company pivots completely. The leader with a setback reinvents their entire approach. The organization facing disruption dismantles established systems.

But **sustainable transformation isn't about starting from scratch; it's about integration.** It is the quiet art of weaving together what has worked with what is being learned, of honoring where we have been while opening to what we are becoming.

When I speak with clients, I tell them that integration begins with better questions. What parts of my past still hold wisdom that I need today? Which strengths once protected me but now need to be reimagined? How do my challenges become part of my power instead of something to hide?

I have lived these questions deeply. The precision that once made me an effective attorney now shapes how I build transformative experiences for others. The cultural duality that once felt like a burden has become one of my greatest assets, allowing me to hold multiple perspectives at once. Even my time in prison, which I once believed would forever define me as an ex-felon, has become one of my greatest teachers. It grounds my empathy, my patience, and my understanding of what it truly means to rise through it.

Nothing is wasted when we commit to integration instead of chasing perfection.

I learned this truth in one of the most unexpected ways, through crochet. When I began making Maya's and Kyler's blankets in prison, the first rows were uneven, the tension all wrong. My instinct was to pull it apart and start again, but Patricia stopped me. "Keep going," she said softly. "The blanket will tell your story. The beginning will be a little messy; the end will be smoother. That is what makes it beautiful."

Her words stayed with me. The blankets became more than gifts for my children. They became proof that even the imperfect parts of our story belong. Each loop, each stitch, each uneven row carried its own truth. Together, they formed something whole and human.

That is the essence of integration. We do not erase our imperfections. We weave them into the fabric of who we are becoming, allowing every mistake, lesson, and victory to add texture and depth. In that weaving, we find beauty not in perfection but in presence.

THE EMBODIED LEADER CREATES LASTING IMPACT

The most profound business insight I've gained isn't about strategy or systems; it's about embodiment. The evolved leader is the embodied leader. It's not just what you know; it's who you are that leaves a legacy.

In executive circles, knowledge is currency. Leaders invest in advanced degrees, specialized training, and constant information consumption. Yet I've observed that the most impactful leaders aren't necessarily those with the most impressive knowledge; they're those who most fully embody their values and vision.

I experienced this distinction personally. Before my fall, I possessed extensive legal knowledge and business acumen. But knowledge alone isn't embodiment. True embodiment happens when values move from intellectual understanding to lived experience.

Now, when I speak about decision-making, resilience, or authentic leadership, I'm not just sharing information; I'm offering wisdom earned through lived experience. There's a resonance that comes from embodiment that information alone can never create.

I see this in the organizations I work with. Companies spend millions on values statements and culture initiatives that remain intellectual exercises, words on walls rather than behaviors in hallways. The gap between knowing and embodying is where most transformation efforts fail.

Leaders who embody their values don't need to reference the mission statement; they are the mission statement in motion. They do not have to enforce cultural norms because they model them naturally. They do not rely on long lists of policies to guide behavior because their integrity inspires alignment through example.

This kind of embodiment creates a different form of influence. People follow an embodied leader not because of title or authority, but because of presence. Because of authenticity. This is not soft leadership. It is the most powerful kind there is.

My own journey of becoming continues through daily practices that keep me rooted in purpose rather than performance.

I begin each morning with intention. The gratitude journal practice I started in prison still anchors me. Three things I am grateful for. Three things that would make today great. Three affirmations that remind me who I am becoming. This ritual shifts my focus from achieving to aligning before the day even begins.

I measure success differently now. It is no longer about accolades or appearances. Success is about depth. How deeply did I connect? How honestly did I show up? How fully did I serve rather than seek approval? Who did I touch and inspire today?

I nurture creativity through singing, dancing, and movement. These are not hobbies. They are sacred reminders that creation does not just happen in work or words, but in the rhythm of being alive.

I practice the pause. Before I react, before I decide, before I speak, I pause. That pause is where wisdom lives. It is where I find freedom to choose with intention rather than instinct.

Presence has become my greatest power. When I step on stage, I am fully there. I am not thinking about my next line or how the audience sees me. When I sit with my children, I am wholly with them. No phone. No emails. Just presence. Because I have learned that people may forget your words, but they never forget how your presence made them feel.

I practice vulnerability. Each time I share my story, I strengthen that muscle. It is not about confession. It is about connection. Each time I speak the truth of my fall and rise, I give others permission to face their own.

I stay rooted in my spiritual practice. The prayers and meditation that held me through my darkest nights still ground me today. They remind me that my purpose is bigger than my pain.

I invite reflection from others. I ask for feedback regularly from those who see me most clearly. It keeps me honest, humble, and awake to my blind spots.

I write to remember. Journaling helps me trace patterns and progress that would otherwise slip by unnoticed.

These are not just personal habits. They are professional practices. They are how I evolve as a leader, a parent, and a human being. They are how I strengthen my capacity to rise not just through the storms I have survived, but through whatever comes next.

When I first came home from prison, I still led from my wounds. I was quick to defend, eager to prove, and terrified to be misunderstood. Over time, as healing deepened, those wounds became scars. They stopped bleeding. They started teaching. They became evidence of my journey rather than anchors to my past.

That shift from wounded to healed changes everything. Wounded leaders create wounded cultures. Their unhealed pain becomes policy. Their defensiveness becomes team tension. Their fear becomes control. Their shame becomes silence.

Healed leaders create something else entirely. Their scars become wisdom. Their vulnerability becomes permission for others to be real. Their resilience becomes cultural strength. Their self-acceptance becomes the soil for innovation and belonging.

The presence of a healed leader is unmistakable. You can feel it in the room. There is calm. There is steadiness. There is a quiet confidence that comes not from perfection but from truth.

This kind of transformation is not mystical. It is the deepest kind of professional growth there is. It happens through reflection, through honest feedback, through courageous self-inquiry. It happens when leaders stop hiding their scars and start using them as beacons.

My own story of shame, failure, and redemption has not disappeared. It has become the heart of my leadership. What once felt like the end has become the beginning of everything that matters most.

"BEYOND SUCCESS" MINDSET

"Success is a terrible teacher," I tell a room full of high-achieving executives. "It rewards what works while hiding what it costs. It convinces us we've arrived when we are still becoming. It answers 'what' but never 'why.'"

I know this truth not as theory but through the unraveling of my own life. By every external measure, I had made it. I had the education, the career, the recognition, the life that looked perfect from the outside. But beneath that image was a silence I refused to face. I was moving so fast I did not have to feel. The applause drowned out the questions whispering inside me.

At what cost was I achieving? Whose definition of success was I chasing? What was I trying so desperately to prove, and to whom?

When the illusion of success finally shattered, I was forced to confront those questions. My fall was not just the loss of a title or career; it was an invitation to rediscover purpose beyond performance. Transformation showed me that real success is not about achievement but about alignment. It is not about being admired but about being of service. It is not about perfection but about presence.

This shift changes everything. It redefines the questions we ask as leaders and as human beings. How am I serving rather than succeeding? What impact does my presence have on the people around me? Am I growing, or am I just getting ahead? Where am I creating meaning that endures beyond the metrics?

Presence is where this deeper truth lives. True presence, the kind that is steady and undistracted, is more powerful than any strategy. When we are fully here, we see what others overlook. We hear the quiet truth beneath the noise. We create space for honesty, belonging, and possibility. That kind of presence changes teams, families, and entire cultures.

When leaders embrace this shift, organizations transform from the inside out. The focus moves from short-term wins to long-term purpose. Fear loosens its grip. Creativity returns. People stop performing and start participating. What emerges is not just a more successful organization but a more human one.

I often tell leaders that this awakening happens in one of two ways: through conscious choice or through crisis. My path was the latter. Losing everything forced me to rebuild from the inside out. But we do not have to wait for collapse to choose growth. Every moment offers a chance to stop chasing and start aligning.

Perhaps the greatest surprise of my journey has been discovering that I am a bridge. I bridge the boardroom and the prison yard. I bridge my Indian roots and my American identity. I bridge success and failure, strength and surrender, intellect and intuition.

Being a bridge is not about perfection. It is about presence. It is about standing in the space between worlds and refusing to choose one over the other. It is about listening deeply enough to hold contradictions without needing to resolve them. In this fragmented world, that capacity to connect, to integrate rather than divide, is the leadership we need most.

The most powerful leaders are not the ones with flawless records. They are the ones who have been broken open and learned to lead from truth. They are the ones who can see both sides and still build the middle ground. They know how to create wholeness out of fragmentation because they have lived it.

My evolution continues.

I am still that fallen child learning to rise. I am still the professional redefining what it means to contribute with integrity. I am still the mother learning that presence matters more than perfection.

Every day, I rise again. Not to prove. Not to perform. But to live, to serve, to love, and to lead from the truth of who I have become.

LEADERSHIP LESSONS: RISING INTO MY PURPOSE

1. **The healed self leads differently.** Leaders who do their inner work, facing shadows and choosing authenticity over appearance, transform organizations. They lead from self-knowledge rather than a need to prove their worth, making decisions without requiring universal approval. When leaders heal their wounds instead of projecting them onto teams, trust deepens and innovation accelerates.
2. **Integration, not perfection.** Sustainable transformation weaves together what worked with what's being learned. The most effective leaders integrate their full story, including failures, rather than hiding challenges. Nothing is wasted when we commit to integration; past setbacks become unique sources of wisdom and connection.
3. **The embodied leader creates lasting impact.** True leadership impact comes from embodying values, not just knowing them. Embodied leaders don't reference mission statements; they are the mission in motion.

They create influence through presence and authenticity rather than position, inspiring aligned action through consistent example.

4. **"Beyond success" mindset.** Success can validate current approaches without revealing hidden costs. Transformative leaders operate where contribution matters more than achievement and purpose supersedes performance. This shift moves organizations from exhausting excellence to energizing purpose, increasing innovation as fear decreases.

REFLECTION QUESTIONS

- What unhealed wounds might you be projecting onto your team, and how could transforming these into wisdom change your leadership approach?
- Where is the gap between what you know intellectually and how you actually show up as a leader? What would it look like to more fully embody your stated values?
- How might you redefine success based on contribution and presence rather than traditional achievement metrics? What small daily choices could move you toward this "beyond success" mindset?

EPILOGUE

Living in the Frame

Nine years after walking out of Coleman Federal Prison Camp, I stand at the edge of a conference stage, watching a room full of executives absorb what I have just shared. Their faces tell a familiar story: the moment when the mask of perfection begins to crack, and light starts to pour in.

"When you let go of who you think you're supposed to be," I tell them softly, "you finally make space to become who you were always meant to be."

A decade ago, I could not have imagined this life. Standing before thousands of people, speaking about courage, vulnerability, and truth. Helping leaders find their voices. Guiding others to rise through their own falls. Transformation never takes us where we expect to go. It takes us where we need to be.

The path from that prison cell to this stage was anything but straight. It was not about bouncing back to who I was. It was about integrating every version of myself: the immigrant's daughter chasing achievement, the high-powered attorney, the convicted felon, the prison teacher, the mother rebuilding trust. Each identity, each chapter, stitched together into something whole and human.

When I visit Kyler at the University of Florida, I see the young man he has become. Confident, driven, and kind. He leads with integrity as president of his fraternity, pours his energy into campus life, and talks about wanting to become a criminal defense lawyer like David. Sometimes I want to wrap him in my arms and tell him he doesn't need to prove anything to anyone, that my love for him is already complete. But I also know that some lessons must be learned, not told.

Kyler carries a fire that both inspires and worries me. His drive is relentless, a mirror of the same intensity that once ruled my own life. Watching him lead, achieve, and push himself to the edge fills me with pride, but beneath it, I sometimes see the flicker of exhaustion that I once mistook for purpose. I recognize the pressure in his shoulders, the unspoken belief that being strong means never slowing down.

When we talk, he tells me about his fraternity events, his classes, the organizations he's leading. I listen, smiling, celebrating every win with him. But in my heart, I pray that he'll one day discover the peace that comes not from doing, but from being. I hope he learns sooner than I did that worth isn't measured in titles or achievements, but in how gently we can hold ourselves through imperfection.

There are moments when I see glimpses of that awareness in him, like light breaking through the armor. In those moments, I know he's finding his own rhythm, one that will carry him further than striving ever could. He is still becoming, as am I.

Maya, my radiant Maya, greets the world with the same open heart that once clung to me as a little girl in the visiting room at Coleman.

She carries a quiet power that humbles me. On the collegiate volleyball court at Trinity College, she moves with determination, fierce yet fluid, a reflection of the strength that comes from knowing both struggle and resilience. But it is her heart that astonishes me most. She feels everything—others' pain, their joy, their unspoken hopes—and somehow still manages to hold her own center. She has learned to lead not by force, but through compassion, creating space for others to rise alongside her.

At Trinity, Maya has faced moments that tested her resolve. Balancing the demands of academics, athletics, and the invisible weight of her own expectations has not been easy. Yet she has learned to navigate those challenges with courage, grace, and a deep trust in her own strength. I have watched her transform fear into fuel, turning uncertainty into growth and setbacks into stepping stones. Each time she doubts herself, she remembers who she is and where she comes from. She breathes, she steadies, and she rises.

What fills me with awe is how Maya carries the lessons of our shared past without letting them define her. She does not run from the shadows of our story. Instead, she stands in the light of her own becoming. She has turned what could have been pain into empathy, what could have been shame into purpose. In her eyes I see not just resilience, but renewal. She has become a woman who knows that vulnerability is not weakness; it is the birthplace of courage.

There are moments when I watch her from afar and feel time fold in on itself. I see the little girl who once searched my face through glass now standing tall, grounded in her own truth, unafraid to be seen. She is both my mirror and my masterpiece, proof that love can rewrite any story. Maya reminds me every day that our past may shape us, but it does not have to limit what we become. Her life is a living prayer that even through heartbreak, beauty can rise.

When I see Maya laugh with her teammates, comfort a friend, or push through exhaustion to chase a dream, I realize she is everything I once hoped to become. She will soar in whatever direction she chooses because her wings are not fueled by ambition alone. They are lifted by heart, anchored in purpose, and guided by love.

The RISE Framework that grew out of my journey now lives in boardrooms, retreats, and coaching sessions. I have watched rooms transform when leaders stop performing and start being real. Reframing is not an intellectual exercise; it is an act of courage. When a CEO stops seeing a market challenge as a threat and starts seeing it as a chance for innovation, everything changes. When a team redefines failure as data instead of defeat, creativity comes alive.

Identifying the people who hold us accountable and lift us higher is not just personal work; it is strategic. I have seen organizations evolve when leaders choose truth-tellers over comfort, diversity over sameness, mirrors over applause.

Surrender is the hardest practice. Especially for those who built entire identities on being the most capable, the most prepared, the most in control. But the greatest freedom comes when a leader finally says, “I don’t know, but I’m willing to learn.” In that moment, their humanity becomes their strength.

And evolution, that sacred, messy, ongoing process, is where everything begins again. It is not a clean story of redemption or a perfect arc of success. It is the daily work of becoming. It is the courage to shed the armor, to lead with presence, to live with truth. I have seen leaders drop the act, teams open up, cultures breathe again.

Nine years after my release, I still stumble. I still catch myself performing. I still feel the pull of old fears. But now I recognize those moments as invitations to practice what I teach. To remember what matters. To rise again, not through perfection, but through presence.

My law license is gone, but my purpose has expanded far beyond any courtroom or title. What I do now is not a career; it is a calling. It is how I serve. It is how I live.

The most beautiful part? I no longer walk alone. Each time I tell my story, someone steps forward to tell theirs. The executive hiding financial stress. The leader carrying shame. The woman afraid to speak her truth. When one person opens their heart, it gives everyone else permission to do the same. We rise together.

Recently, I found an old photograph from the holidays. In it, my parents, my children, and Erik stand beside me. The joy in our faces is not performance but peace. Erik and I have built a new rhythm as co-parents, one rooted in mutual respect and deep love for our children. When we gather as a family now, it feels whole in a way that perfection never could.

I am finally living in the frame.

The fall that once felt like the end became the foundation for everything real. Not because I am extraordinary, but because I am human. Because I stopped hiding. Because I chose to rise.

And that is what I want others to know. Your darkest moments can become your greatest teachers. Your deepest pain can become your most powerful contribution. Your failures can become your legacy.

The question is not whether you will fall or whether you will struggle. You will. The question is whether you will rise through it, and who you will become in the process.

We were never meant to be perfect. We were meant to be real.

And in that realness, in that raw and radiant truth, we find not just our own liberation but the courage to lift others.

That is my legacy now. Not a perfect image, but a life fully lived. A story of rising through it all, again and again, with courage, with purpose, and with the power to be real.

YOUR CALL TO ACTION

Now it's your turn.

This book isn't just a story to read; it's an invitation to rise.

Whatever challenge you're facing, whether it's a public failure, a private struggle, or the quiet dissatisfaction that comes from living a life that looks good but doesn't feel authentic, you have everything you need to rise through it.

Start where you are with what you have.

STEP 1: REFRAME YOUR CHALLENGE.

Take the situation you're currently facing and write three different ways to see it. What if this isn't happening to you, but for you? What might become possible if you viewed this as an opportunity rather than an obstacle? How might this challenge be preparing you for your next level of impact?

STEP 2: IDENTIFY YOUR SUPPORT SYSTEM.

Map the people who form your foundation. Who are your truth-tellers, the ones who will reflect reality back to you, even when it's uncomfortable? Who are your supporters, the ones who believe in you even when you've lost belief in yourself? Who are your challengers, the ones who push you to grow beyond your comfort zone?

Reach out to at least one person from each category this week. Share something real. Ask for what you need. Create space for authentic connection.

STEP 3: PRACTICE SURRENDER.

Identify one area where you're gripping too tightly, trying to control outcomes, maintain appearances, or resist reality. For just one week, experiment with letting go. What happens when you release the need to know exactly how things will turn out? What becomes possible when you stop performing and start being real?

STEP 4: COMMIT TO EVOLUTION.

Choose one daily practice that will support your ongoing transformation. It might be meditation, journaling, creative expression, or intentional connection. What matters isn't the specific practice but your commitment to continuous growth.

STEP 5: SHARE YOUR STORY.

As you begin to rise through your own challenges, share what you're learning with others. Not once you've figured it all out or overcome it completely, but in the messy middle of your own becoming. Your vulnerability creates permission for others to be real about their struggles too.

Most importantly, remember that rising isn't a solo achievement; it's a collective practice. We need each other's stories, support, and wisdom to navigate our own journeys of transformation.

The world doesn't need more people pretending to be perfect. It needs more people with the courage to be real, to acknowledge both their wounds and their wisdom, to share both their falls and their rising.

That's how we change not just our own lives but our teams, our organizations, and our communities.

One authentic story at a time. One courageous choice at a time. One act of rising at a time.

I'm rising through it. Will you join me?

About the Author

Rashmi Airan is a former Ivy League–educated attorney and Wall Street investment banker whose life took an unexpected turn to federal prison. What began as a moment of downfall became the foundation of a global movement. Today, Rashmi is a sought-after transformation expert, entrepreneur, and speaker whose RISE Framework helps leaders and organizations turn adversity into fuel for growth, resilience, and purpose.

A first-generation American with an unshakable belief in second chances, Rashmi's story challenges comfort zones and sparks bold conversations about integrity, belonging, and the courage to rebuild. Her debut book, *All Rise*, is a raw and unforgettable invitation to step into vulnerability and rise through it.

She calls Miami home and rocks a sneaker collection as bold as her message.